Nigel Edley is a leading scholar of
together his insights from 25 years of
book that provides an excellent int
recommended for anyone who w
masculinity today.

Rosalind Gill, *Professor ..... and Social Analysis,*
City, University of London

Men and Masculinity: The Basics is a great read – superbly connecting
academia to everyday life. Edley takes us skillfully through a wealth of
cases, research reports and anecdotes, opening sites of tremendous
controversy and contention, leaving us with a deeper understanding –
and even some optimism for cultural change.

Michael Bamberg, *Professor of Psychology,*
Clark University

MEN AND MASCULINITY

THE BASICS

Men and Masculinity: The Basics is an accessible introduction to the academic study of masculinity which outlines the key ideas and most pressing issues concerning the field today. Providing readers with a framework for understanding these issues, it explores the ways that masculinity has been understood in the Social Sciences and Humanities to date. Addressing theories which view masculinity as being in a permanent state of flux and crisis, it explores such problem areas as:

- the male body
- men and work
- men and fatherhood
- male sexuality
- male violence.

With a glossary of key terms, case studies reflecting the most important studies in the field of masculinity research and suggestions for further study, *Men and Masculinity: The Basics* is an essential read for anyone approaching the study of masculinity for the first time.

Nigel Edley is a senior lecturer in social psychology at Nottingham Trent University, UK. He has published extensively in the field of masculinity studies, including *Men in Perspective: Practice, Power and Identity* (with Margaret Wetherell).

The Basics

For a full list of titles in this series, please visit www.routledge.com/
The-Basics/book-series/B

MEN AND MASCULINITY
NIGEL EDLEY

MUSEUM AND GALLERY STUDIES
RHIANNON MASON AND
ALISTAIR ROBINSON

DISCOURSE
ANGELA GODDARD AND NEIL CAREY

LANGUAGE, GENDER AND SEXUALITY
SARA MILLS

CHOREOGRAPHY
ERICA STANTON

MODERNISM
LAURA WINKIEL

INTERNATIONAL TRADE
JESSIE POON AND DAVID L. RIGBY

WORLD THEATRE
E.J. WESTLAKE

GLOBAL JUSTICE
HUW L. WILLIAMS AND CARL DEATH

CRITICAL THINKING
STUART HANSCOMB

MORMONISM
JOHN CHARLES DUFFY AND
DAVID J. HOWLETT

TRAGEDY
SEAN MCEVOY

RELIGION IN AMERICA
MICHAEL PASQUIER

FOLKLORE
SIMON J. BRONNER

MEN AND MASCULINITY
THE BASICS

Nigel Edley

Routledge
Taylor & Francis Group

LONDON AND NEW YORK

First published 2017
by Routledge
2 Park Square, Milton Park, Abingdon, Oxon OX14 4RN

and by Routledge
711 Third Avenue, New York, NY 10017

Routledge is an imprint of the Taylor & Francis Group, an informa business

British Library Cataloguing in Publication Data
A catalogue record for this book is available from the British Library

Library of Congress Cataloging in Publication Data
A catalog record for this book had been requested

ISBN: 978-1-138-79036-0 (hbk)
ISBN: 978-1-138-79037-7 (pbk)
ISBN: 978-1-315-76424-5 (ebk)

Typeset in Bembo
by Sunrise Setting Ltd., Brixham, UK

In memory of Sarah Smart

CONTENTS

FIGURES

ACKNOWLEDGEMENTS

I would first like to thank various members of the editorial staff at Routledge for their interest, expertise and patience – from Andy Humphries, through Siobhan Poole and Iram Satti to Alyson Claffey, who saw me over the finishing line. I would also like to register my appreciation for the support of the School of Arts & Humanities at Nottingham Trent University, especially for the period of sabbatical leave that helped to get this project off the ground. I am indebted to Margie Wetherell, Clare Tomlinson and my daughter, Laurie, for their willingness and diligence in reading through various drafts. Last, but certainly not least, I must say a big 'thank you' – and sorry – to Clare, for putting up with a man who keeps the most unsociable of working hours.

PART 1

MAN-WATCHING

I am sitting on a campsite in Switzerland's magnificent Saas Valley, resting from the rigours of a day spent in the mountains. In a neighbouring pitch, a man and a woman are busy organising their belongings, preparing to leave the site. They are travelling by motorcycle and a startling amount of equipment has been laid out on the ground, ready to be packed away. There's a quiet efficiency about the way they approach the task (they've been through this routine many times before). Both set to work putting things in bags, strapping them together and attaching them to the bike – which grows ever more impressive in stature. In less than half an hour everything has been put away and they are ready to hit the road. They zip into their leathers and put on their crash helmets. I wait for him to take the handlebars and for her to perch herself on the seat behind him. They do precisely that – before zooming off down the valley.

On 1 October 2012, a five-year-old girl is reported missing from near her home in a small village in mid Wales. Two days later, her mother makes an appeal on national television asking for anyone with any information of her daughter's whereabouts to contact the police. In the following days, police and search-and-rescue teams scour the local area looking for signs of the missing child. Hundreds of people from the same area give up their time to join in with the search – which was to become the largest missing persons operation in UK police history. On 5 October, a police spokesperson announces that the case has become a murder enquiry. I know that the killer will be a man. On 30 May 2013, Mark Bridger is found guilty of the abduction and murder of April Jones.

In the wake of the publication of *The Decline of Males*, the anthropologist Lionel Tiger and the feminist critic Barbara Ehrenreich enter into a discussion about the state of men (and women) on the eve of the twenty-first century. Their conversation is featured in the June 1999 edition of *Harper's Magazine* – and it struck me as being a highly gendered exchange. See if you can identify who is who from the following (abbreviated) extract:

A: I want to explore your feelings about these things. You say the 'decline' of males – there's a sad tone to that. I would feel sad, as a [parent] of a son, if males suddenly started 'declining' in some serious way. Do you feel loss and regret and nostalgia?

B: I'm not interested in characterizing my own personal psyche in this matter, solely because I think it's of zero interest to anyone. What is of interest is the fact that, as you suggested, young men and women are very concerned about these matters, one reason being that they no longer have a set of rules that they think are emotionally and morally worthwhile. [B expands].

A: You certainly got away from the issue of how you feel about it. See, I'm willing to say how I feel.

B: I'm wholly uninterested in your feelings.

In the course of doing the research for this book, I encountered a paper by the psychologist, Anna Machin (Machin, 2015) in which she described an established psychometric test, called the YIPTA (short for the Yale Inventory of Parental Thoughts and Actions), which is used for measuring the strength of the bond between parents and their children. The inventory includes a fairly long list of actions that are conceived to be indicative of a healthy attachment: the existence of routines around feeding and bedtime; daydreaming about the baby's future and the creation and repeated use of special nicknames. However, it is another key indicator which catches my attention: 'thinking that one's baby is the most beautiful in the world'. I jot down in my notes: 'Since when was rampant irrationality a sign of good parenting?'

I'm travelling towards the coast on a Bank Holiday weekend and, predictably, the traffic on the road is heavy. Rarely do I get above third gear. The line of vehicles in which I am situated is constantly on the move, but it's a frustrating case of repeatedly speeding up and slowing down for what seems like hours on end. But in my wing mirror I can see someone making slightly quicker progress. Several hundred yards behind me is a car that is weaving in and out of the line of vehicles. Taking every opportunity of a gap in the flow of oncoming traffic, the driver is engaged in a series of overtaking manoeuvres, leapfrogging two or three vehicles at a time. Some of the other drivers are clearly less than impressed by the actions of this road-user. Two or three have already flashed their headlights in annoyance at having to provide refuge from the prospect of a head-on collision. Eventually it comes to my turn to be overtaken. I glance sideways as the car races past, knowing that I'll see a man behind the wheel. But I don't. Instead it's a young woman, eyes fixed forwards, singing away to something on the radio.

We live in a world that is manifestly gendered. Turn on the television, open up a newspaper or simply walk down the street and there they are: men and women, boys and girls, plain for all to see. Generally speaking, it doesn't take much to distinguish one from the other; indeed, we can often spot the difference at a glance – even from a distance. The tell-tale signs are many and varied. We usually make up our minds on the basis of how people look, move and act. Of course, it is not unknown for us to get tripped up once in a while, to occasionally make the wrong 'call'. But for most of the time we seem to be quite successful in our gender discriminations, as evidenced by the fact that we tend to remember those occasions when our intuitions are confounded rather than confirmed. Yet in spite of the apparent obviousness of gender, there has been a tremendous amount of debate amongst academics about how to make sense of this most ubiquitous feature of human societies. There have been sharp disagreements about the very nature of gender, arguments about the mechanisms by which people become gendered and divided opinions too about the prospects or possibilities of refashioning gender in various ways. However, one of the most striking features of *Gender Studies* is that, for many years, the focus was really just on *women*. It was they who were seen as interesting or exotic – in need of explanation. Men, by contrast, seemed like fairly unremarkable creatures; they came across as being just ordinary, normal, 'nothing to write home about'. This *normalisation* of masculinity was brought home to me, both powerfully and awkwardly, early on in my research career. At the beginning of the 1990s, I was working on a project which involved interviewing men about different aspects of their lives, such as work, family and friendships. In the very first meeting, I decided to open with a question about what they understood by the term 'masculinity'. It was met with stony silence. I tried to rephrase the question to give them more time to think; this time it was greeted with a bout of nervous laughter. After what seemed like an age, one of the men eventually piped up: 'it isn't really a subject you think about consciously before you ask the question'.

One of the pioneers of masculinity research – the American sociologist Michael Kimmel – can offer us another anecdote that helps both illustrate and explain this tendency for men's gender to go unnoticed or unmarked.[1] Kimmel was in a postgraduate study group discussing feminist issues, when an argument broke out between two female participants: one white, the other black. The white woman had just claimed that all women were bound together by their common plight under **patriarchy**, but the black woman disagreed. She asked: 'When you wake up in the morning and look in the mirror, what do you see?' The white woman replied that she saw a woman in the mirror. 'That's precisely the issue', said the other, 'I see a black woman'. She then went on to explain how her ethnicity was part of her everyday consciousness, whereas, for white women, their colour was invisible because they were (and still are) privileged in that respect. Kimmel was profoundly struck by this exchange because he realised that when he looked at himself in the mirror, not only had he failed to see his whiteness, but he had also failed to see his gender. What confronted him was just the image of a person – an ordinary human being. It was, for him, what one might call a consciousness-raising experience. It was as if, from that point onwards, Kimmel was bound to see the world through somewhat different eyes. In 1987, he would go on to produce one of the earlier books on men and masculinity, but he was by no means the first man on the scene.

THE EMERGENCE OF *MEN'S/MASCULINITY STUDIES*

It is often difficult to pinpoint the origins of an intellectual tradition. Even where an obvious candidate might exist, such as in the cases of *Marxism* or *Confucianism*, the reality is often much more complicated, involving all kinds of formative influences and antecedents. Tracing the origins of *Men's Studies* is by no means a simple task. The current entry on *Wikipedia* describes it as 'a relatively new field of study' – and with some justification, as a high proportion of the books and articles written about men and masculinity have appeared at some point during the last thirty years. That said, some critics would argue that scientists and philosophers have been writing about men and masculinity for centuries, rather than just a few decades. It certainly isn't difficult to find older books with 'men' or 'man' in the title; to single out just two examples, the anthropologist Ralph Linton published *The Study of Man* in 1936 and, earlier still, there was Charles Darwin's *The Descent of Man*, which first appeared in 1871. Of course, neither author would have accepted the charge that they were ignoring half of the human race. Both would have seen themselves as using the so-called 'male generic', where 'man' is shorthand for men *and* women. In more recent years, however, the use of the male generic has come under critical scrutiny. It has been suggested that the convention is far from innocent or benign. Critics argued that the image of humankind promoted over the centuries by scientists and philosophers has been decidedly male. We now know that Aristotle saw the human body as a male body, with the female form as something of an aberration. It is now widely recognised that Sigmund Freud, the father of psychoanalysis, regarded femininity as a failed form of masculine identity. Classical sociology has its own examples of this same leaning. Famously, Karl Marx called for the workers to rise up and throw off their chains; but in his imagination this was to be a revolution of male miners, labourers and factory workers, not mothers and housewives. The critics claimed that, like Kimmel's own reflection, men have long been held up as the definitive human being against which women are compared, contrasted and, where found different, usually seen as lacking.

As many will no doubt have anticipated, it was feminists who were at the forefront of advancing these criticisms. In the 1960s and 70s, **second wave feminists** were not only complaining about the **androcentrism** of Western culture but were also busy establishing the field of *Women's Studies*. This new discipline was set up to provide a platform for women's voices and to explore their lives and experiences *as* women. But what it also did, albeit inadvertently, was to usher in its male counter-part. It is easy enough to see the influence of feminism on the emergence of *Men's Studies*. All one needs to do is to look at some of the earliest titles to appear on the scene: *The Liberated Man* (Farrell, 1974), *Men's Liberation* (Nichols, 1975) and *A Book of Readings for Men against Sexism* (Snodgrass, 1977) – the hallmarks are unmistakable. The influence for some of these writers was intimate, stemming from their relationships as friends, brothers and husbands of feminist activists. They took on board and extended the (liberal) feminist idea that gender was a straitjacket from which people needed to escape. In 1976, Herb Goldberg wrote *The Hazards of Being Male* and, in so doing, joined a small chorus of other writers in claiming that an adherence to the norms and expectations of the 'male sex-role' (Chapter 2) was damaging men's health and happiness (see also Fasteau, 1974; Pleck and Sawyer, 1974; Harrison, 1978). The feeling amongst such authors was that men had as much to gain as women, perhaps, from a sexual revolution. Not only would it open up their horizons to experience and explore more feminine modes of being, but it would also relieve them of some of the more arduous – even toxic – aspects of being a man, such as the need to always appear tough, aggressive and brave in the face of danger (Brannon, 1976).

However, the subtitle of Goldberg's book – *Surviving the Myth of Male Privilege* – reveals another way in which the second wave fuelled the fire of *Men's Studies*. For every man inspired to join his 'sisters' in their struggle for liberation, there would be at least one other who was left feeling bemused, angered or threatened by their campaigns. Like others that would follow (for example, Bly, 1990), *The Hazards of Being Male* didn't so much try to refute feminist claims about the plight of women as highlight the injuries incurred by men within traditional gender arrangements. But, as we can see from the subtitle, Goldberg had no sympathy for the more radical suggestion that men were the chief architects and main beneficiaries of women's suffering. As far as he was concerned, patriarchy was a myth. In the intervening years, a number of other authors have continued to push this particular theme but in a way that is often much more directly critical of feminist orthodoxy (see Faludi, 1992, for a discussion of this 'backlash'). Writers such as Lyndon (1992), Farrell (1994), Hise (2004) and Benatar (2012) have gone so far as to suggest that it is in fact *men* who are now the subordinated sex – which is a claim also found in the rhetoric of various Men's Rights groups, which have sprung up in various parts of the world, including the US, India and Australia.

There is no little irony about the fact that feminism provided a key spur to the development of *Men's Studies*, because many feminists are highly sceptical about the whole enterprise. In *Women's Studies: The Basics*, Bonnie Smith (2013) asks why, as a society, we need yet more attention paid to men, when they have dominated the spotlight for such a long time? Understandably, writers like Smith are wary of men wanting to 'get in on the act'. The fear is that, even where their intentions seem good, men have a tendency to end up dominating proceedings. Like inviting a man on a girl's night out, inevitably the dynamics change. Almost inexorably, he becomes the focal point of the evening, dictating the flow of topics and dominating the conversational floor (Spender, 1980; Fishman, 1978). Undoubtedly, tensions have been increased by the use of the label *Men's Studies*. For obvious reasons, people are drawn to imagine that this must be the male equivalent of *Women's Studies*, which has made no secret of the fact that it is dedicated to the advancement of women's position in the world. By extension, therefore, people tend to assume that *Men's Studies* seeks to further the lot of men. Moreover, in the case of writers like Neil Lyndon and David Benatar, such fears appear to be well founded; and yet there are many others working within the same area who pursue a very different politics. Indeed, the most prominent names in the field – Connell, Kimmel, Messner and Pleck – would all align themselves much more closely with the perspectives of feminist scholars. In response to this rather complex political landscape, some of these academics have abandoned the title *Men's Studies* in favour of an alternative nomenclature – that of *Masculinity Studies*. This is also my preferred designation. Like Kimmel, it is used to signal work that not only treats men *as* men, but which also sees them as operating in a complex field of gender relations in which they are usually privileged.

Feminism has had a major impact on both *Masculinity Studies* and the lives of men more generally – not least in terms of how it has changed their mothers', wives' and sisters' (etc.) ideas and expectations about what is right and just in the way of gender relations. But it is not alone in providing a stimulus to academic interests in men. Another key factor has been the rapid transformation of the whole political and economic landscape over the course of the last forty years. In that time, Western economies have shifted from being production-based, industrial societies to post-industrial 'consumer societies' (Goodwin *et al.*, 1997). In much of Europe and America, this period has seen a sharp decline, not just in the traditional 'heavy' industries, like mining and steel, but also across much of the manufacturing sector. In today's world, a much greater proportion of working people are employed either within service industries or in jobs that involve the handling and manipulation of information. The fact that so many jobs these days revolve around *communication* (for example, telephone or computer-based), rather than *making* things, has led some sociologists to talk about the *feminisation* of work (Richer, 2012). Moreover, the same time period has witnessed a feminisation of the *workforce*, too. For instance, since the 1970s, the UK has seen a 20 per cent fall in the number of men in paid employment, coupled with a comparable rise in the proportion of women in work, such that, by 2016, there was close to parity in terms of the balance of the overall workforce. As we will see later on in this volume, work has often been at the very heart of what it means to be a man. As such, any major disruptions to established patterns of labour were always likely to have a significant impact on the lives and sensibilities of men.

THE CRISIS DEBATES

Irrespective of whether the focus is upon work or some other aspect of men's lives, the growth of masculinity studies has been greatly accelerated by a pervasive understanding that all is not well with the male half of the population. Indeed, there has been much talk of men being in a state of *crisis*. Again, witness the titles of the following publications: *Predicaments in Masculinity* (Rutherford, 1992), *Masculinity in Crisis* (Horrocks, 1994), *The End of Masculinity* (MacInnes, 1998), *Uncertain Masculinities* (O'Donnell and Sharpe, 2000), *Redundant Masculinities?* (McDowell, 2003). The British psychotherapist Anthony Clare began his own book *On Men* by declaring: 'At the beginning of the twenty-first century it is difficult to avoid the conclusion that men are in serious trouble' (Clare, 2000: 3). Of course, one doesn't need to trawl through academic texts in order to hear about the trials and tribulations that beset the modern man. For years now, the media have been replete with stories of impending or unfolding crises. For example, in January 2014, the national press in the UK warned (again) that young men were becoming a 'disadvantaged group' in higher education, after figures revealed that considerably more girls than boys were both applying for and attaining places at UK universities.[2] The statistics suggested that, over the last twenty-five years, this 'gender gap' in educational achievement was continuing to widen – and it also seems to apply to almost every subject across the school curriculum, including maths and science. Similar trends have been noted in other industrialised areas of the world – including the United States[3] (NB the trend is often reversed in poorer countries, where girls may have relatively limited access to education). Another focus for concern in recent years has centred upon men's health. In many cultures around the globe, men are well known for their reluctance to seek help for both physical and mental ailments, but in the West, too, there have been claims that society tends to discriminate against men in terms of things like the amount of research funding dedicated to male-specific illnesses, such as prostate cancer (Farrell and Sterba, 2008). Since 2004, the global profile of men's health has been raised by the '**Movember**' campaigns (which originated in Australia but can now be observed across Europe, South Africa and the Americas[4]). The UK's Movember website notes that whilst men are significantly less likely than women to call upon mental health services, they are also three times more likely than women to take their own lives. Indeed, in the UK, death by suicide has become the leading cause of death in men under the age of 35.[5] All the evidence points to the fact just that as many women as men *attempt* to commit suicide, but because men use more deadly or violent methods, their chances of 'succeeding' are considerably higher.

As we shall see towards the end of this book (Chapter 7), the association of men and violence is very well established in the academic literature. Indeed, all around the world, concerns are being voiced about the rise in violent crime perpetrated almost exclusively by men. During the writing of this book, the world's most famous Paralympian, Oscar Pistorius, has been in the dock, defending a charge of murdering his own girlfriend. The media coverage surrounding the court case has served to shed light on the alarming level of gun crime in South Africa. Despite having a population that is significantly smaller than the UK, South Africa sees in excess of 15,000 murders every year, approximately thirty times higher than the level in the UK.[6] Many of these killings have been attributed to the actions of urban gangs competing over the trade in illegal drugs. According to *Reuters*,[7] the Central American countries of Honduras and Venezuela have the highest murder rates in the world, driven up, once again, by drug-related 'turf wars' between rival gangs. The UK, by comparison, has a much lower profile with respect to gang crime – although it was blamed by some government officials for the rioting that took place on the streets of London (and some other major city centres) during the summer of 2011.[8] I mention this last point not out of any sense of national pride, but because it links to yet another purported area of crisis: one of those same government officials blamed the spread of gang culture in the UK on the problem of absent fathers.[9] Fatherhood, like violence, will be the focus of a dedicated chapter (Chapter 5) in the second part of this book, but it is worth pointing out here that, as with violence, there have been long-standing concerns expressed about men's fulfilment (or not) of their parental roles and responsibilities. Since the 1990s, there has been a distinct swing away from the idea that a good father is simply a breadwinner or provider for his family. These days, there is a much greater emphasis on fathers 'being there' for their children – and yet, according to some sections of the media (at least), this is another arena in which men are running into difficulties. One UK newspaper, reporting on the results of a national survey, claimed that twenty-first-century dads are feeling increasingly stressed, depressed and disappointed with their experiences of family life.[10] Another links the crisis to the phenomenon of 'family annihilation', where fathers murder all of their own children in a single killing event.[11]

A final example (for now) of the crisis thesis concerns an issue that links fatherhood back to the state of men's health. In the last few years, scientists have been warning that, all around the globe, men's fertility is in sharp decline. Reports have suggested that, since 1990, average sperm counts have fallen by as much as a third.[12] It seems far from clear what might be causing this dramatic effect; explanations have ranged from the impact of industrial-scale use of fertilisers in agriculture to overly tight underwear! Over roughly the same time period, medical (and media) attention has also been focused on the incidence of erectile dysfunctions. Not only is the prevalence of such disorders significantly higher than was previously imagined (especially amongst the over-40s), but the proportion of younger men reporting difficulties is also said to be on the increase. One by-product (or buy product!) of this trend is a multi-billion-dollar trade in Sildenafil – or Viagra, as it is more commonly known. It is now thought to be one of the world's most widely taken drugs, having been used by an estimated 20 million men.[13] It is claimed that many young men have become psychologically addicted to Viagra.[14] It is said that in an age where most boys learn about sex via internet pornography, they are particularly vulnerable to feelings of 'performance anxiety', and it seems that, for many, Viagra (or one of its commercial competitors) has become almost indispensable in their attempts to manage those anxieties.

Whilst a lot has been written about these different facets of the so-called crisis, there has also been a good deal of debate about the validity of the whole thesis. Some commentators remain largely sceptical, seeing it either as an invention of the media or as a sign of men wanting to re-establish themselves as the centre of public attention (see Segal, 2007, for a short review). However, there is also some dispute about what the crisis actually means. It is possible to illustrate the main point of contention by reference to the front cover of Roger Horrocks' book (Figure 1.1) – which, in 1994, was one of the first to adopt the vocabulary of crisis. As we can see, the cover features the image of a man with his head in his hand. Here, surely, is a man in crisis – and yet that's not the title of the book. It refers to something rather different. Horrocks called his book *masculinity* in crisis, not men in crisis. What, we might ask, is the difference? Probably the easiest way of exploring this issue is via the use of a concrete example. I noted just a moment ago that, in today's world, more emphasis is placed on fathers 'being there' for their children. In times gone by, fathers were seen as much more marginal to their day-to-day care and management. In the UK, during the first half of the twentieth century, the delivery room of the maternity ward was generally thought to be an inappropriate place for the prospective father. The usual practice was for him to wait elsewhere whilst the mother gave birth to the child. And yet, at the beginning of the twenty-first century, all of this has been turned upside down. Today, expectant fathers risk exposing themselves to the staunchest of criticisms if they opt not to be by their partner's side. In 2010, for example, the ex-Liverpool-footballer John Barnes was widely denounced for staying at work whilst his wife was in labour. Much more common these days are reports of international sportsmen taking time out from competition in order to be present at the birth. In 2011, the Australian cricketer Ricky Ponting flew home from an overseas tour of Sri Lanka in order to be with his wife. Years ago, there would have been audible mutterings that he was letting down his country and his teammates; but such complaints were conspicuous by their absence.

So, wherein lies the crisis? Is it in the figure of Barnes, who, for some, displayed an unforgivable lack of care and concern for his wife and new baby? Is it in the shape of men like Ponting, who feel compelled, however willingly, to fly nearly half way around the world, as one American sports journalist put it, 'just to say hello to someone you'll be seeing for the rest of your life'? It has to be said that in neither case did the man involved seem particularly wracked by anxiety or uncertainty; neither was spotted with his head in his hands. In fact, both men seemed very much at ease with their own decisions. Seen in this way, the crisis would consist not so much in terms of the traumatisation of individual men but as the disruption

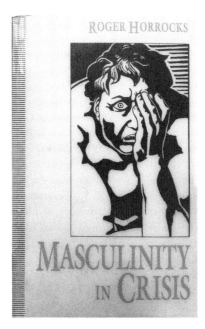

Figure 1.1   Masculinity in Crisis cover

Source: © Roger Horrocks.

and resettlement of cultural ideas about what is right and proper for a man to do and be. Today's men might say (and truly believe) that they wouldn't contemplate missing the birth of a child; but just a few generations ago, they were saying, just as honestly, that they would happily be elsewhere. As this book will repeatedly demonstrate, the contours of gender change over time. Indeed, according to Michael Atkinson (2011), the history of masculinity shows it to have been in a state of perpetual flux. He would argue, I think, that in any era people are prone to exaggerate the significance of the times in which they live. It's easy to imagine that life 'back then' was so much more settled, solid and predictable, whereas the likelihood is, of course, that every period has its own measure of disruptions and dilemmas. Nonetheless, there do seem to be some grounds for thinking that the last thirty years have been amongst some of the more turbulent times in the history of men and masculinity, even if, perhaps, not uniquely so. The challenges thrown down by second wave feminism and the turmoil brought about by the forces of **globalisation** (in particular, the spread of **neo-liberalist** politics) means that men are living their lives in the context of radical change. The crisis, if it exists at all, is surely their attempts to deal with a scene of rapid transformation.

What is beyond question, however, is the fact that over that same thirty-year period there has been a remarkable expansion in the scope and scale of academic writing about men. Back in the mid 1990s, Margaret Wetherell and I wrote a book on men and masculinity, which sought to provide an inter-disciplinary review of the field at that time (Edley and Wetherell, 1995). To attempt to do the same thing today would represent a formidable, if not impossible, task. Ten minutes spent browsing through *Google Books* is enough to prove the point. There, one can find literally hundreds of books on men and masculinity, most of which have appeared in recent years. In the first ten or so webpages I counted just six titles published before 1995, three times that number between 1995 and 1999 and double that figure again between 2000 and 2005. All kinds of angles and aspects have now been covered. Should you wish to do so, you can now find books that focus on Canadian men, New Soviet men and Oxbridge men; you can read about Christian masculinities, prison masculinities – even female masculinities. At the same time, there are now three academic journals dedicated to the study of men and masculinity: the *Journal of Men's Studies* (established in 1993), *Men and Masculinities* (established 1998) and the *Psychology of Men & Masculinity* (established 2000). The field of *Masculinity Studies* has truly come of age.

THE STRUCTURE OF THIS BOOK

This book is divided into two parts. This chapter and the next make up Part 1 and are designed to lay the foundations for the thematic chapters which follow in the second half. Chapter 2 is dedicated to matters of theory – which is, in some respects, a calculated risk, because it may tempt some readers to skip straight to Part 2 and the promise of more tangible fare. However, I would really like to encourage readers not to be so tempted; partly because I think that the theoretical arguments around men and masculinity are themselves quite fascinating, but also because, as I try to explain in Chapter 2, it is very difficult to consider any aspect of men's lives outside the bounds of theory. Indeed, I have taken this risk to enable readers to more easily identify the theoretical undercurrents of work found in the masculinities literature and to provide a sharper picture of the differences and commonalities that exist across those theoretical framings. The bulk of Chapter 2 is given over to a discussion of five different approaches to understanding men and masculinity. It will look at arguments suggesting that masculinity is a function of biology, a state of mind, a trained response, an effect of power and, finally, a practical accomplishment or performance. In each case, my aim is to give those respective arguments a 'fair hearing', although they will be critical reviews in which my own opinions and preferences are bound to shine through. I trust that there will be a more than sufficient number of references to the alternative arguments for those who wish to explore those controversies further.

Part 2 begins with a chapter that focuses on the subject of the male body. Like most of the others in this section, Chapter 3 aims to situate the body within a historical context – to examine its shifting significance over time. It looks at how male bodies have been recruited and disciplined by the state and how, in more recent times, they have become the centrepiece for many men's sense of identity or selfhood. The chapter explores some of the ideological tensions that surround men's relationships with their own bodies and looks at how they try to manage those contradictions. The discussion touches on the significance of the body for a range of different men, including gay men, older men and those with physical disabilities. In closing, it also looks at the role of sport as an institution and considers one of the more popular forms of body modification – tattooing.

Work is the focus of Chapter 4. As noted earlier, dramatic shifts in the structure of global economic systems have been identified as the source of destabilisation and stress in the lives of millions – but especially in the case of men, given the close connections between masculinity and the role of the breadwinner. This chapter examines the nature of those links and looks at the ramifications of these radical transformations. What has not changed is the fact that the world of work remains a highly gendered domain. However, it is not just a case of men and women doing different kinds of job. As will be explained in this section of the book, academics have shown not only that institutions can be gendered (as well as people), but also that the practices of work can be seen as implicated in the very production of gendered selves. In Chapter 5, we turn our attention to the subject of fatherhood. As numerous commentators have pointed out, governments and various other official bodies have placed great emphasis upon the importance of fathers in helping to maintain stability in both the lives of their families and in society more generally. In this chapter, we will be looking at men's engagement with their own families as well as trying to capture and convey what fatherhood means to them, both emotionally and symbolically. We will consider the impact of parenthood on fathers themselves and also look at the significance of fatherly input on the health and happiness of both their sons and daughters. Chapter 6 takes us into a discussion of male sexuality. As I mention at the start of that section, Freudian psychology has often been the prime resource for trying to make sense of men's erotic activities, but this chapter takes a more historical perspective (in common with the rest of Part 2). It sets out to trace the philosophical and ideological underpinnings of contemporary sexuality – in part, through the concept of *sexual stories* (Plummer, 1995) – in order to show how our cultural heritage both shapes and inhabits the most private or intimate aspects of men's lives. As with the discussion of fatherhood, I place particular emphasis on trying to explore and expose men's lived experiences of sex, to reveal its social and emotional *significance*. The chapter also looks at both straight and gay masculinities as well as at attempts to blur or dismantle that distinction. Unfortunately, there's an all too obvious link between the themes of male sexuality and *male violence* – which is the focus of the final chapter of Part 2. In Chapter 7, we will look at some of the ways that societies encourage men to be violent – particularly within the contexts of war and sport. It will also examine the phenomenon of US college campus shootings, such as at Columbine and Virginia Tech, as a way of trying to understand some of the complexities of these appalling acts. Following the contours of the wider literature on this topic, we will tease out some of the differences between male-on-male violence, violence against women and sexual violence. In so doing, the discussion will draw upon research findings from countries as far apart as Africa, South America and Europe.

In looking forward to the chapters that make up this volume, I would like to make a couple of final points. In the preface of Raewyn Connell's (2009) book on gender (see *Further reading*, below), she notes that *Gender Studies* is now a global phenomenon. Moreover, she makes a conscious effort to seek out and showcase not just information about the relevance of gender for people found on all five continents, but also the gender scholarship that derives from those different regions. In this volume, however, I have been less concerned with trying to 'balance the books' in this way. In other words, my reviews of the literature tend to reflect the fact that a preponderance of the current research on men and masculinity both stems from and relates to the situations found in North America, the UK and the Antipodes. The second point is also about difference. Once again, Connell has been at the fore in explaining that masculinities are *manifold*, rather than singular or unitary. As well as geographical variations, there are distinctions to be made between black, white and Latino men, straight men and gay men, old men and young men, able-bodied and disabled men as well as men from the whole spectrum of socio-economic classes. Across the seven chapters of this book, we will touch upon all of these different categories. However, academics working in the social sciences and humanities talk about *intersectionality* – or the interplay of different factors (Hill Collins and Bilge, 2016). Kimmel's anecdote about the dispute between the two feminists was, in essence, a lesson about intersectionality – the fact that gender and ethnicity interact in such a way that undermines any easy alliances between women (or, indeed, between whites or blacks). There are references to such intersectional research in this volume (most conspicuously in Chapter 6). However, it doesn't require a mathematician to work out that it is simply impossible – in a lifetime of research, let alone a little book – to cover all of the bases. Those six factors alone would generate literally thousands of permutations. This book has been written to offer you the *basics* in terms of what we know about men and masculinity. There is a wealth of additional information out there for the interested reader, as well as an awful lot of research that still remains to be done.

NOTES

1 https://www.ted.com/talks/michael_kimmel_why_gender_equality_is_good_for_everyone_men_included?language=en (retrieved 14 August 2016).

2 http://www.telegraph.co.uk/education/educationnews/10608739/Boys-being-left-behind-as-university-gender-gap-widens.html (retrieved 2 July 14).,

3 http://en.wikipedia.org/wiki/Educational_attainment_in_the_United_States (retrieved 2 July 14).

4 http://en.wikipedia.org/wiki/Movember (retrieved 2 July 14).

5 http://www.ons.gov.uk/ons/taxonomy/index.html?nscl=Causes+of+Death (retrieved 2 July14).

6 https://africacheck.org/factsheets/factsheet-south-africas-official-crime-statistics-for-201213/ (retrieved 2 July 14).

7 http://uk.reuters.com/article/2014/04/10/uk-latam-crime-idUKBREA390IK20140410 (retrieved 20 April 14).

8 http://www.theguardian.com/politics/2011/aug/11/new-gangs-drive-signalled (retrieved 3 July 14).

9 http://www.theguardian.com/uk/2011/oct/01/gangs-ukcrime (retrieved 3 July 14).

10 http://www.theguardian.com/society/2004/jun/20/childrensservices.uknews (retrieved 3 July 14).

11 https://www.theguardian.com/uk-news/2013/aug/11/masculinity-crisis-family-murder (retrieved 3 July 14).

12 http://www.independent.co.uk/news/science/scientists-warn-of-sperm-count-crisis-8382449.html (retrieved 3 July 14).

13 http://digitaljournal.com/article/334150 (retrieved 3 July 14).

14 http://www.dailymail.co.uk/femail/article-2212529/Addicted-Viagra-They-virile-growing-number-young-men-t-cope-little-blue-pills.html (retrieved 3 July 14).

FURTHER READING

Connell, R.W. (2005) *Masculinities* (2nd. edition). Cambridge: Polity. Connell stands as one of the leading lights in the field of men and masculinity studies – and this book (published originally in 1995) was a seminal moment. It was a decisive turn in thinking about masculinities as both plural (rather than singular) and hierarchical.

Connell, R.W. (2009) *Gender: In World Perspective*. Cambridge: Polity.

  This is a bold attempt, in so short a book, to look at gender (not masculinities specifically) in a global context. Connell looks at lives outside of what she calls the *metropole* (i.e. the most 'developed' parts of the world: North America, northern Europe and the Antipodes) and also highlights some of the gender scholarship that has emerged from those often neg lected regions.

Kimmel, M.S. and Messner, M.A. (eds) (2012) *Men's Lives* (9th. edition). Boston: Allyn & Bacon.

  The fact that this book is in its ninth edition testifies to its enduring appeal. It is a large compendium of articles arranged into different sections by theme. Some of the contributions are new whereas others are (often abridged versions of) the classics. The most common themes include boyhood, work, friendships, sexualities and future gazing.

Segal, L. (2007) *Slow Motion: Changing Men, Changing Masculinities* (3rd. edition). Basingstoke: Palgrave.

  There is no shortage of general introductions to the field of men and masculinities, but they vary a good deal in terms of their quality and sophistication. This is certainly one of the best. First published in 1990, Segal offers an incisive but sympathetic critique from a feminist perspective, including chapters on fatherhood, ethnicity and men's violence.

Smiler, A. (2004) 'Thirty Years after the Discovery of Gender: Psychological concepts and measure of masculinity'. *Sex Roles*, 50(1): 15–26.

  This is a succinct account of the emergence and subsequent development of the field. It documents the shift from thinking about masculinity to masculinities and also the move towards more qualitative, rather than quantitative, approaches to the subject.

COMING TO TERMS WITH MEN AND MASCULINITY

In any field of academic enquiry it is vital that one begins with a clear understanding of the key terms that anchor and structure the main lines of debate. For instance, in sociological discussions around social class, it is obviously crucial that people know and agree upon what they *mean* by the concept of class – otherwise there will be all too much room for confusion. Within this book, therefore, we need to establish what we mean by the concepts *men* and *masculinity*. Now, as we saw in the first chapter, this can prove to be more difficult than one might anticipate. People may go around under the general apprehension that they have a firm enough grasp of the sense of these two notions, but when push comes to shove, there is every chance that they will find themselves confounded. Again as we saw earlier, of the two terms, the meaning of *masculinity* seems the most likely to prove elusive, but that's not to suggest that there are no complexities around the concept of *men*.

In embarking upon this task, it's important to note that there's an extra dimension to these discussions, one that gives them a particular sense of urgency. The key theme here is that of *change*. The much talked-about crisis of masculinity is all about change. Feminism – in all of its guises – demands that men change their ways to accommodate the rights of women. The shift from industrial to consumer societies also demands that men must change – at least if they are to thrive in modern times. In a sense, the very notion of 'crisis' speaks of the difficulties of change: can men do it? Can they transform or reinvent themselves anew? The answer to that most fundamental question depends upon the nature of men and masculinity. What ties men to their distinctive ways of being? Is it instinct, custom or simple determination? Those are the issues at stake in the discussions that make up this chapter.

INTERROGATING COMMON SENSE

Amongst the books in this series, there are titles dedicated to topics such as Literary Theory, Eastern Philosophy and Bioethics. It is easy to imagine readers coming to those texts with little or no prior understanding of what they are about to encounter. The same cannot be said, of course, for a book on men and masculinity. As I pointed out at the start of the opening chapter, we live in a world in which the existence of men (and women) is taken utterly for granted. People appear to be highly adept at recognising the distinctive hallmarks of men and masculinity. What is there still to find out? Isn't it all just a matter of common sense? By the time you reach the end of this chapter, you will be aware that quite a lot of academic writing about men and masculinity flies in the face of everyday thinking. But let us begin by putting the spotlight on our common sense and examining what it has to offer in terms of arguments and insights.

Think about this: when we spot a 'man' out on the street, what exactly are we recognising? For the vast majority of readers, the key to any answer will orientate around the sense of that person as *male*. Any 'man', we might assert, is *necessarily* male. But is that it? Are men just males, plain and simple? Well, not really – insofar as common sense also tells us that some males don't seem very 'manly' or masculine. Someone who appears weak, timid or ineffectual might strike us in this way. Common sense also contains the idea that certain experiences can *make a man* of somebody. The prospects of travelling the world or becoming a father are the kinds of things that evoke such sentiments – and yet, clearly, in neither instance would there be any sense of the person in question becoming any more *male*. The 'making' of a man in these kinds of everyday reference is a matter of *character* and *conduct*, rather than anything to do with the physical body. That said, common sense does posit the idea that there are links between these different facets of masculinity. In many parts of the Western world (at least), it is assumed that men's behaviour is often the *product* or *consequence* of their being male – that men cannot help but act the way they do because that is 'just the way they are built'. Once again, though, the picture is far from simple. In everyday life, the idea of men as slaves to their own nature sits fairly easily alongside the suggestion that masculinity is something that can be inculcated or stifled – that masculinity is as much an impression from *outside* as an expression from within.

As we reflect upon our common sense we should see that it offers a surprisingly rich and complex array not just of assumptions about the nature of men and masculinity but also of *theories*. One of the first lessons that I try to instil within my own teaching on gender is that it is almost impossible to talk about men and masculinity without invoking some kind of theory. Students often seem to think that theories sit outside common sense, as something formal (and difficult!), but the fact is that it is replete with theories or attempts to make sense of everyday life. Let me offer an example to help demonstrate that point. Back in 1993, a two-year-old British boy called Jamie Bulger was lured away from his mother's side, whilst they were out together shopping. He was led along a busy street and then beaten to death on a nearby railway siding. On learning of this tragedy, what most shocked the British public was not just the brutality of the attack but the age of the assailants. Jon Venables and Robert Thompson were, at that time, just ten years old. The ensuing outcry showed that whilst people may have come to anticipate that men are behind most acts of abduction and murder, they don't expect the culprits to be of such a tender age. Young lads might get themselves into a bit of mischief ('boys will be boys') – fighting, falling out of trees, knocking on neighbours' doors and then running away – but they don't commit murder. Significantly, in the trial that followed it was claimed that the perpetrators might have been corrupted by a particular 'video nasty' (*Child's Play 3*). It was suggested that the film might have drawn them into copying some of its more grisly scenes. As it turned out, this claim was later dismissed by the court. Nevertheless, we can see that this suggestion, like the other speculations, was predicated on certain theoretical notions. The idea that 'boys will be boys' clearly invokes the assumption that males are predisposed towards acts of an anti-social nature – that it is somehow normal or expected for them to test the boundaries of what is seen as acceptable. Likewise, the allegations surrounding *Child's Play 3* trade on theory, albeit of a very different order. Here boys *learn* how to behave in gendered ways. It is the same kind of theory which deters many parents from buying their sons toy guns and swords for Christmas. Such things are seen as a bad influence. Of course, other members of the same family might think quite differently. 'You can't stop boys liking guns' they'll say, 'Go on, let him have one!' Whether it is a national outrage or just a private family dispute, what fuels the fire of debate in both cases is a clash of theoretical positions.

The main purpose of this chapter, therefore, is to put the spotlight on theory and to look at what academics have had to say about the nature of men and masculinity. That said, in reviewing this literature, we will not be leaving common sense entirely in our wake. In the social sciences and humanities, academic theory and common sense have quite a close relationship: everyday ideas often inspire and form the basis of formal theories, and those formal theories sometimes make it back into common sense via the media, the classroom and volumes such as this. There is, in other words, a circulation of ideas between academia and everyday life. For instance, it is not at all uncommon these days to hear people describing modern men as 'more in touch with their feminine side'. Such expressions trip off the tongue. But where does this notion come from? It's not a simple fact that men have such a thing; rather, this is yet another example of a bit of 'theory-talk'. So, in taking a more critical look at some academic theories, the hope is that we might also gain some insights about the intellectual heritage of some of our own everyday thinking.

THE NATURE OF MASCULINITY: FIVE THESES

As has been mentioned already, there is now a very substantial literature dedicated to the subject of men and masculinity. In amongst it all there are many different theories and concepts; indeed, it is well beyond the scope of this book to attempt anything like a comprehensive or thoroughgoing review of the full range of ideas. Therefore, the way that this chapter will be organised is around a single – and ostensibly simple – question: what is the actual *substance* of masculinity? As suggested by the header above, we are going to consider five distinctive answers to that question, each coming from a different theoretical perspective. Taken together, these framings cover the dominant theoretical approaches to the study of men and masculinity.

MASCULINITY – AS AN EXPRESSION OF THE BODY

The first thesis that we will set out to explore orientates around the widely held conviction that masculinity is, in one way or another, an outward expression of the condition of being male. Of course, the feasibility of any such notion rests upon how we understand or define that state or condition. What, exactly, does it mean to be a male? Now, of all the questions posed within this book, this is surely one for which we might think common sense can supply a perfectly adequate answer. Everybody knows that, all across the globe, the sexing of newborn babies is based upon a cursory inspection of the infant's genitals. That is, the midwife or attending physician just has to look between the baby's legs and, depending upon what they find there, declare the child to be either a boy or a girl. Isn't it as simple as that? Well, no, it isn't. In reality, this describes just one of at least *four* different ways of defining and/or determining a person's sex. The issues involved here are not only complicated but also highly contentious.

Consider the much publicised case of the South African athlete Caster Semenya. Semenya first came to prominence at the African Junior Championships in 2009, when she produced a series of world-class performances in both the 800m and 1500m. Such was the manner of her dominance that rumours began to spread casting doubts about her status as a female. In response, the International Association of Athletics Federation (IAAF) asked Semenya to submit herself for testing. Significantly, their procedures around 'gender verification' do not consist of just a two-minute stripsearch (as used to be the case, back in 1950, when the IAAF first introduced mandatory sex-testing). Rather, Semenya would have had to undergo a whole battery of tests, including physical examinations, tissue sampling and psychological screening – with the results emerging not over the course of minutes but of days or even weeks. That such investments of time and effort are involved speaks volumes about the difficulty and delicacy of the judgements being made.

The difficulties begin with the fact that there is not one but (at least) three different physical dimensions of sex. That is, a male can be defined according to (1) genital anatomy (i.e. a penis rather than a vagina), (2) internal sex organs or *gonads* (i.e. testicles rather than ovaries) and (3) genetics (i.e. XY sex chromosomes rather than XX). Of course, there wouldn't be an issue if these three dimensions were always perfectly aligned or co-extensive, but the plain fact is that for some individuals this simply isn't the case. For instance, it is unusual, but possible, for a person to be born with female genitalia and yet have XY chromosomes. It is also uncommon, but possible, for a person to have XX sex chromosomes and yet be born with what appears to be a penis. Some people are born with *both* ovaries *and* testes. Others are born with a mixture, or 'mosaic', of XX and XY chromosomes – and some are born with a different combination (or *karyotype*) altogether, such as XYY or XXY. As a conservative estimate, in a country the size of the UK, one might expect around 1000 babies per year to be born into one or another of these conditions (Fausto-Sterling, 2000). The question is: how are we to regard their sex?

For many years, the most common 'solution' was to privilege, or enforce, one particular dimension (usually the external genitalia) and then, as far as possible, to attempt to bring the rest of the body 'into line' – often through invasive surgical procedures. More recently, however, there has been a move towards seeing sex as a matter of *self-determination* (this is the fourth definition). In other words, it is assumed that people have a profound sense of their own *identity* as male or female – even where, as is the case with many transsexuals, that sense of self is at odds with the physical dimensions of sex. Hence, today, parents and medical teams are often urged to wait until the individual in question is old enough to decide for themselves. The third alternative is even more radical. Organisations such as the UK Intersex Association (www.ukia.co.uk) argue that people shouldn't have to decide. They look to challenge the very assumption that everyone must be either male or female. The reality of sex, they argue, is not black and white – and a great deal of misery and anguish result from society's attempts to shoehorn people into either one of these two sex categories.

If we accept that being male is a *multifarious* condition, we can still ask questions about how the various bodily or physical dimensions might help shape or even determine the contours of masculinity. So, in the same order as above, let's start by considering what role the penis might play. As many anthropologists and cultural historians would be able to testify, some extravagant claims have been made, over the years, regarding the power of the human penis (or *phallus*), but very few would give much credence to the idea that it stands as the driving force behind things like the murder of Jamie Bulger or such acts of reckless driving as described at the start of the book. A penis might well be a remarkable little organ, capable of quite dramatic transformations in terms of its size and appearance, but it doesn't have that kind of reach or degree of agency! The penis may play a central role in the initial ascription of sex, but it can't be considered as the font of masculinity. Its status is more like the mane of a male lion or the fantail of a peacock. It's more of a *sign* than the source.

The next item on our list takes us from the penis to men's *testicles*. In many Spanish-speaking regions of the world, people use the phrase *tener cojones* (literally, 'to have balls') in response to displays of particular courage or bravado. It may well be a euphemism, but it does at least hint at a link between men's bodies and their behaviour. If such a connection does exist, then the form it would take is a particular product of the testes – the hormone **testosterone**. As a matter of fact, testosterone is not exclusive to men; it is also found in the bodies of females, as a product of both their ovaries and adrenal glands. However, it is the case that males produce considerably higher levels of testosterone – especially during the early period of foetal development and during puberty. The effects of testosterone on the male body are now well documented. During puberty, for example, it promotes things like the growth and strengthening of bones, the development of facial hair and the twin delights of body odour and greasy skin. In contrast, there is much more in the way of speculation when it comes to trying to assess the impact of the same hormone on men's behaviour. One of the most commonly heard claims is that increased levels of testosterone result in a greater tendency towards aggressive behaviour amongst men, but the fact is that the evidence is far from conclusive (Turner, 1994). One of the reasons why it has been so difficult to pin things down is that the human body responds to environmental conditions by regulating the production of hormones. So, for example, if a boy takes up some sort of vigorous activity, such as boxing or weightlifting, his body will respond by creating more testosterone to help facilitate the repair and building of his muscles. In other words, there seems to be a reciprocal relationship between testosterone and men's behaviour, rather than a 'one-way street' of cause and effect.

The same arguments apply in relation to a parallel set of debates about supposed differences between men's and women's brains (Naftolin, 1981; Moir and Jessell, 1989; Einstein, 2007). With the development of new imaging and scanning technologies has come a veritable torrent of research studies looking for sex differences in brain physiology and functioning. It has been claimed, for example, that there are differences in the thickness of the outer layer (or cortex), in the balance of 'white' and 'grey' matter and in the number of fibres that connect the two hemispheres. Some scientists have suggested that these differences arise in the womb, as a result of differential exposure to foetal testosterone. However, later research seems to suggest that they may be postnatal developments (Jordan-Young, 2010; Fine, 2010): that is, something that emerges in response to (or in 'dialogue' with) social and environmental conditions. Either way, many hours have been spent trying to imagine how such differences might connect with or 'cash-out' in terms of masculine and feminine behaviour – but without, it has to be said, a great deal of success.

Like hormones, our genes would also appear to offer some obvious potential as a bridge between men's bodies and their behaviour. In recent years, there have been tremendous developments in the field of genetic science – from the completion of the **Human Genome Project** (in 2003) to the manufacture of disease-resistant GM (genetically modified) crops, and great strides made too in the development of various gene therapies. In amongst all of this research, there have also been a few claims made in relation to men and masculinity – the most conspicuous being speculations around the existence of an 'aggressive' gene and another said to control the proclivity to rape. As Cordelia Fine (2010) points out in her book *Delusions of Gender*, readers new to this kind of research are easily cowed (and impressed) by the technical jargon. It all seems so *scientific* that, surely, it has to be true. However, as she goes on to demonstrate, the studies behind the headlines are not always what they seem. Sometimes, the science itself is highly dubious; at other times, it is more a case of idle sensationalism on the part of those who broadcast the news of these studies. For example, in the last few years, there have been at least two new stories announcing the 'discovery' of aggressive genes: the so-called 'macho' (or SRY) gene found on the Y chromosome and another dubbed the 'warrior' gene, located on the X. Both were heralded as offering explanations for why men are more aggressive than women. But read below the headlines and one finds a rather different story. For instance, in the latter study, the lead researcher reported that only one per cent of people (NB all people, not just men) carry the 'warrior' gene – and also that its impact was mitigated by particular social factors. The idea that the cause of male aggression had been found seems seriously wide of the mark.

Even more doubtful are the claims made about the existence of a 'rape gene' in Thornhill and Palmer's (2000) book *A Natural History of Rape: Biological Bases of Sexual Coercion*. From the outset it is important to note that, whilst Thornhill is a biologist and Palmer an anthropologist, the book itself is a work of evolutionary psychology – the stock-in-trade of which involves trying to the deduce, from a Darwinian point of view, what adaptive potential might exist in various forms of human behaviour. So, in this case, the 'logic' would be that, because rape is so prevalent a phenomenon, it must be, in some way, 'hardwired' into at least some men's genetic code. Furthermore, they would contended that, in evolutionary terms, rape has proven to be a 'successful' behavioural strategy for men, in the sense that rapists have been able to propagate their genes (including the purported rape gene) through both acts of rape and normal, consensual, sex. Ironically, the same kind of 'logic' can be applied to men's aggressive driving. We might ask: why do men engage in such risky behaviour? One would think it directly *counter*-productive to the chances of propagating of one's genes. However, for the evolutionary psychologist, there is almost always an answer. They would simply claim that, over the course of evolution, the willingness to take risks must have proved itself to be profitable. It takes a bold man, perhaps, to go around seducing the wives of his peers – and/or, maybe, throughout the ages, women have found daredevils particularly sexy or alluring (although why they might do so would require its own line of evolutionary logic). However, there are serious problems with all of these genetic explanations. Evolutionary psychology has been roundly (and rightly) criticised for its lack of testability (mainly because it involves *post hoc* theorizing, i.e. working *backwards* from results to explanations) and also for its chronic conservatism ('whatever the status quo, it must be so for good reason') (Buller, 2005; Wallace, 2010). As for the claims about macho and warrior genes, most genetic scientists agree that there is no one-to-one relationship between traits and genes – even for the most simple of physical features, like hair or eye colour. So, the very idea that there may be specific genes controlling complex social behaviours – like excessive drinking, sexist banter and the penchant for fast-action crime thrillers – is not one that most would care to entertain.

MASCULINITY – AS A PSYCHIC STRUCTURE

If masculinity is not an expression of the male body, then what else could it be? In this section, I want to explore the idea that it is a powerful *state of mind*. For the most part, we are going to be concentrating upon the claims put forward by probably the most famous psychologist of all time – Sigmund Freud. However, towards the end of the section, we will move on to consider some other ideas that take Freud's work as their point of departure. There's a veritable library of writings about Freud and the psychoanalytic tradition he founded, and, needless to say, we can only sketch the broadest of outlines here. Nevertheless, for those unfamiliar with the man and his legacy, it is worth starting with a little bit of background to Freud's story before going on to look at what he had to say about the nature of men and masculinity.

Freud was born in 1856 and spent his childhood in Vienna. At the age of seventeen, he went to his home-town university to study medicine with a particular interest in neurology. He qualified as a doctor in 1881 and spent the next few years doing research on various brain disorders. In his late twenties, Freud had just taken up a position as a lecturer in neuropathology when he visited Paris to see a French neurologist called Jean-Martin Charcot, who was looking into the use of hypnosis with patients suffering from **hysteria**. The encounter changed the course of Freud's whole life. What he saw was that people could be transformed under hypnosis. Patients suffering from neurotic disorders – like the paralysis of limbs or the inability to speak – could move and talk when put into a trance. People could remember things that they couldn't recall in their normal state of wakefulness – and people could have ideas implanted into their minds which, upon being brought out of the trance, they would act on and profess as if they were their own. It led Freud to propose a theory of the *unconscious* – which, of course, is a concept with which most readers will be very familiar. Yet it is important not to let our familiarity blind us to radical nature of what Freud was saying about the nature of folk. His arguments did – and still do – present a very serious challenge to a deeply cherished view of our selves as reasonable and rational. Freud claimed that there is much about ourselves that we do not, and perhaps cannot, understand. As you are about to see, he said that people are moved and motivated by powerful irrational forces that are simply too shocking or shameful to be admitted into everyday consciousness.

One of Freud's most controversial assertions was that children are, from the very outset, sexual beings. He claimed that we arrive into the world with an inbuilt drive to seek out sensual or erotic pleasure (in Freud's term, we possess an active *libido*). Pleasure could be derived from a number of different bodily sites or regions, not just from the genitals. For example, he thought that infants gained satisfaction from the acts of sucking, defecating and urinating. As if this wasn't controversial enough, Freud also argued that, from around the age of three, children develop a profound sexual interest in their own parents (or, more accurately, in the parent of the opposite sex). He wrote that little boys come to desire their own mothers – and that they begin to see the father as a rival. Freud went on to claim that, on finding his impulses blocked and his desires frustrated, the young boy starts to becomes anxious that his father will exact upon him some terrible punishment. Indeed, most sensational of all, Freud said that the boy child comes to fear that his father will castrate him. Such is the extent of this anxiety that the boy banishes all thoughts of desiring his mother deep into his own unconscious mind – where they remain, active but invisible, for the rest of his life (Freud labelled this dramatic sequence of events the 'Oedipus complex' – after the Greek myth – where Oedipus is drawn, unwittingly, into killing his own father and marrying his own mother).

Once you've had a chance to catch your breath (!), we need to take some time to consider the implications of Freud's ideas for our understanding of men and masculinity. Freud was firmly of the opinion that the early years of a person's life were crucial in shaping their character. He believed that, to all intents and purposes, their path was as good as fixed from the age of about six. In no small way, Freud saw the boy's emerging personality as marked by the trials and tribulations of the dramas outlined above. In a sense, it represents the scars of battle – not only in terms of the injuries incurred along the way but also in terms of the tactics or strategies that helped him make it through. To a degree, it's an idiosyncratic journey, dependent, in turn, upon the character of his parents and the nature of the family dynamics. However, Freudian theorists would also insist that there are *patterns* in the ways that boys negotiate a path through those perilous years – and it is those patterns that we can think of as different masculinities.

One classic pattern involves the object of men's sexual desires. Significantly, Freud didn't believe that people were naturally heterosexual. Instead, he saw heterosexuality as the consequence or outcome of a (relatively) 'successful' passage through the Oedipus complex. Once established, however, the man's heterosexual career is seen as haunted by the repressed desire for his mother. Deep down, well out of sight or conscious thought, she is the woman for whom he longs – a yearning never to be embraced or admitted but always resonating somewhere in the back of his mind. What can he do, caught, as he is, by the dilemma of being so drawn by the forbidden? Freud claimed that one common attempt at resolution sees men try to separate love from lust.

> Where such men love they do not desire and where they desire they cannot love. They seek objects they do not need to love, in order to keep their sensuality away from the objects they love.
>
> (Freud, 1912: 182–3)

Psychoanalysts call it the 'Madonna/whore complex', whereby men divide women into two opposing categories: those whom they admire and respect and those they would like to take to bed. Since the days of Alfred Kinsey's pioneering research (Kinsey *et al.*, 1948), there have been many reports on the incidence of marital infidelity – which have resulted in some wildly different estimates (Figes, 2013). But what has remained fairly consistent is the suggestion that men are more prone to going astray. Of course, some might see this as evidence of a higher sex drive in men; others might feel that it reflects some kind of moral deficit. But, for psychoanalysts, the tendency is most likely explained as the workings of this complex. In so many marriages, where the woman looks after her husband by preparing his meals and washing his clothes, the resonance with the care provided by his mother might be particularly acute. By this account, it is little wonder that so many men struggle with erectile dysfunctions. Men love their wives – often very dearly, but they somehow do not *want* them. Their lust must find different and safer targets.

According to Freud, another common hallmark of the young boy's passage through the Oedipal drama is a subsequent investment, on the part of men, in the realms of science, art and the production of culture more generally. In his work, Freud wrote about the various methods by which men could defend themselves against the threat of forbidden desires. The process of *sublimation* was one such mechanism, whereby a person redirects their libidinal energies into more wholesome pursuits. Of course, one might wish to contest the suggestion that men are especially productive in the creation of civilization. Feminists would be quick to point out the myriad ways in which women's contributions have been stifled, ignored or written out of history. But psychoanalysts would respond by saying that, whilst sublimation is not exclusive to men (women have their own guilty secrets to forget), in their case it carries a greater intensity, due to the added impetus of their castration anxieties (Frosh, 1987).

Reflecting on the above, it is not hard to see why Freudian psychology has caused such strong reactions. In the eyes of many, it seems completely 'off the wall'. The very idea that boys as young as three entertain lustful thoughts about their own mothers – or that they believe that their own fathers are out to castrate them – sounds utterly preposterous. However, it is important not to be too hasty in dismissing psychoanalytic claims. It is not as if they lack any kind of supporting evidence. For instance, society's presumption of childhood innocence leads many new parents to react with both alarm and concern when they first see their baby boy not only with an erection but engaging in what looks like masturbatory activity (just log on to www.mumsnet.com). Psychoanalysts would also point to the phenomenon of *childhood amnesia*: that is, the fact that people generally cannot recall anything of the events that took place when they were around three or four years old. One might think that these events are hard to remember simply because they happened a long time ago, but that doesn't add up, as many octogenarians can recall their first day at school – but not pre-school. Moreover, ask a six-year-old to recall anything from when they were three and they will struggle, even though, for them, it was not that long ago. Yet, arguably, the most powerful source of evidence lies in people's (hysterical?) reactions to the invitation to imagine having sex with their own parents. It's a rarely asked question but, when posed, most people find that they simply 'don't want to go there' – which, perhaps, does more to support Freud's arguments than it does to undermine them.

There are, however, alternative versions of psychoanalytic theory which move away from some of the more controversial aspects of the Freudian model. One of the most influential variations is Object Relations theory (Greenson, 1968; Chodorow, 1978, 1989). Within this school of thought, much less emphasis is placed upon the sexual aspects of life. Instead, what is said to count most, in terms of how an individual's personality or character unfolds, is the quality of the child's early relationships – particularly with its mother. Object Relations theorists claim that the mother/child bond is like no other. Indeed, they suggest that, in the first few weeks and months of a baby's life, the relationship is so close that their respective senses of self are positively blurred. In terms of the mother, the baby still feels like it is part of her own body, so attuned is she to its rhythms and requirements. As for the child, those early days are experienced, to all intents and purposes, as an extension of its time in the womb. It wants for absolutely nothing. However, it is said that the child's sense of its own self begins to coalesce as it encounters the first pangs of hunger or discomfort. That is, it gradually becomes aware of itself as a separate being or entity via a dawning sense of its own profound dependency.

Object Relations theorists argue that everybody has to go through this process of *individuation* in order to establish a firm sense of identity. However, rather like Freud, they have suggested that the path is different depending upon the sex of the child. For girls, the journey is relatively straightforward. They just have to come to see themselves as similar but separate from their mothers. But for boys, on the other hand, the process is rather more complicated. Not only do they have to arrive at a sense of independence, but they also have to imagine themselves as *different* from the mother. In the formal terminology of Object Relations theory, the boy has to *dis-identify* from his mother and then *counter-identify* with his father (Greenson, 1968). Greenson argues that this double act of identification sets in train what many might regard as the central characteristic of masculinity – namely, its *defensiveness*. He argues that being a man involves a 'flight from the feminine': that is, the male psyche is built around an almost hysterical need or desire to reject anything and everything that is commonly associated with women or girls. Indeed, they would argue that the very meaning of masculinity is a contrast or counterpoint to the realm of feminine things. Interestingly, I have seen some evidence of these patterns in some of my own research. You might recall that I started my first ever research interview with the (show-stopping) question: what do you think masculinity is? When they finally got around to answering, they said things like 'it's the opposite of femininity' and 'it's those aspects which distinguish you from a woman'. Likewise, when they were asked to recall moments in their lives when they felt positively manly, they mentioned things like shaving or lifting heavy objects – in other words, things that women either wouldn't or, perhaps, couldn't do.

As we can see, psychoanalytic accounts of men and masculinity differ very significantly from biological explanations. Nevertheless, neither perspective holds out too much hope in terms of the prospects of change. Whereas biological accounts see masculinity as the playing out of the design of men's bodies, psychoanalytic explanations see it much more as a product of the mind – but a mind that is both soon fixed and highly resistant to most attempts at manipulation (not least because so much of it is simply inaccessible). By comparison, Object Relations theorists do see more scope for change – particularly if men could be persuaded to take a more equal part in the day-to-day care of their own young children (Chodorow, 1989). However, the irony of such a suggestion is that the 'treatment' requires the cure. In other words, within the terms of Object Relations theory, men are likely to remain reluctant to engage in primary childcare when that practice stands as a central plank of the very thing (i.e. femininity) from which they are constantly trying to distance themselves.

MASCULINITY – AS A TRAINED RESPONSE

For all of the ways that psychoanalysis challenged common sense, one thing it didn't do was to disturb the widespread assumption that not only were men and women constitutionally different, but men, in almost every respect, were the superior sex (indeed, some have argued that Freud did much to bolster such a view – for example, Millett, 1972). Women were viewed as more frail, fragile and morally corruptible (Hall, 1992). But as the twentieth century wore on, these assumptions came under increasing pressure – especially after the First World War and with the rise and landmark successes of **first wave feminism**. It was out of this heightened political atmosphere that a young anthropologist emerged who would strike a telling blow against the idea of natural male dominance. Margaret Mead's book *Sex and Temperament in Three Primitive Societies* (Mead, 1935) detailed the behaviour of males and females from three tribes situated in the northern reaches of what is now Papua New Guinea. The truly startling thing about her findings was how different the three cultures were, despite their geographical proximity. In one tribe (Arapesh), she found both males and females to be kind, cooperative and peace-loving. In another (Mundugamor), she found both sexes to be equally hostile, competitive and fierce. It was only in the third tribe (Tchambuli) that she discovered a sharp difference between the temperaments of the men- and women-folk, but it was the opposite of what people in the West would have thought of as typical. In other words, the females of the Tchambuli appeared to be the dominant sex. They were the ones who held council and gave out the orders, whilst the males of the tribe were more likely to be found dancing, making pots and telling each other stories.

As one might imagine, Mead's book caused quite a stir. In particular, it helped to establish the idea that masculinity and femininity were something social or cultural, rather than biological. This was an argument that was steadily gaining momentum by the middle part of the century, partly through the publication of Simone de Beauvoir's (1949) influential text *The Second Sex* (in which she made the now famous declaration that 'one is not born, but rather becomes, a woman') but also with the development of the concept of *sex roles*. **Role theory** itself had already been around for some time (originating in the writings of George Herbert Mead (1934) and Ralph Linton (1936)), but it was in the 1950s that the concept was applied specifically to the behaviour of men and women. The early pioneers were the sociologists Talcott Parsons and Robert Bales (1953). They claimed that, in society, men and women performed different but complementary roles. Men, they said, were *instrumentally* oriented, meaning that they take responsibility for getting things done. Women, on the other hand, were said to perform more of an *expressive* function; that is, they were more concerned with maintaining social cohesion and looking after people's emotional well-being. Of their day, these were progressive ideas – in the sense that the two roles were seen as having a social, rather than a biological, basis. But as the 50s gave way to the 60s, they became viewed as increasingly conservative – not least for the way that they celebrated this role division as being vital for the stability of both the family and society more generally.

The concept of sex roles did not disappear, however, with the failing fortunes of Parson's approach. Indeed, it re-emerged with both new vigour and a new theoretical underpinning, based upon the principles of **social learning theory** (Mischel, 1966; Bandura, 1977). So configured, *sex-role theory* would go on to become the dominant way of understanding the nature of masculinity (and femininity) for the best part of three decades. In fact, one could argue that, in various modified forms, it still stands as the primary theoretical resource or framework for masculinity research today. At the heart of sex-role theory is a very simple premise: men *learn* to become manly. In its purest formulations, it assumes that people start out in life as blank slates (*tabula rasa*), ready and waiting to be marked or inscribed. The process of inscription amounts to a period of intense training, through which young boys come to adopt 'sex appropriate' attitudes and patterns of behaviour. The mechanisms involved are very similar to the ways that one would set about training a domestic pet. If you want to teach your dog to walk to heel or fetch your slippers then, over a period of time, you shape its behaviour towards those goals through a regime of rewards and punishments. When it first picks up your slippers, you ply it with praise and plenty of tasty treats; when it chews them up and buries them in the garden, you banish it to a spell in the doghouse! Gradually, i.e. after several pairs of slippers, and by stealth, it should arrive at the desired mode of conduct.

Sex-role theorists claim that this training takes place in a number of key institutions. The first and, arguably, the most important is the family. Research has demonstrated that parents treat newborn babies in subtle but systematically different ways, depending upon the sex of the child (Rubin *et al.*, 1974; Culp *et al.*, 1983; see also Stern and Karraker, 1989). It has also shown that domestic environments are often shaped in ways that support and help to perpetuate sex-stereotypical behaviour (for example, Rheingold and Cook, 1975). Schools are another important arena. Teachers, these days, are often very sensitive to the issues of gender equality, but again the evidence suggests that subtle forms of sex segregation are still quite common-place (Page and Jha, 2009; see also Delamont, 1995; Hannon, 1981). Another domain which has received a tremendous amount of critical attention is the media (Gill, 2007; Gunter, 1986). Whilst significant efforts have been made, in places such as the UK, to purge public service broadcasting of sexist content, in the case of commercial media, the controls are nothing like as stringent. Whether one looks at the so-called 'size zero' debates (in respect of women's fashion and body image), the controversies surrounding the portrayal of both men and women in hip-hop music or the growing concerns about sexism on digital platforms such as Facebook and Twitter, we find clear evidence of anxieties about the way that people (but especially the young and impressionable) are pressured, policed and pigeonholed into highly particular roles.

But what are these roles exactly? Or, more specifically, what does the male sex role actually look like? According to Brannon (1976), it is made up of four broad elements: (1) *no sissy stuff* – a 'real' man should avoid doing anything remotely feminine. (2) *the big wheel* – a 'real' man is somebody influential. He should be a 'mover and a shaker'. His actions should always matter. (3) *the sturdy oak* – a 'real' man will be strong and dependable. When others are running around upset or in a panic, he will remain a picture of calm. (4) *give 'em hell* – a 'real' man should be fearless in the face of danger. He should have a rebellious streak and, as an opponent, he will appear formidable, even dangerous. Since the publication of Brannon's list, others have offered their own accounts of the male sex role, but most of them are along the same lines. Some have just expanded the list. For instance, Levant *et al.* (1992) claim that there are seven distinctive themes: the four as outlined above plus *stoicism* (or a restrictive emotionality), **homophobia** and an instrumental attitude towards sex.

Of course, irrespective of the details of these portraits, it is important to keep in mind that they are culture-specific. Both of the above profiles come out of a North American context, and whilst they might hold good for other Western societies, they are by no means universal. One only has to think back to Margaret Mead's (1935) famous study to see how norms can vary. But questions of difference do not stop there. As we noted at the very start of this chapter, in any given culture we know that not all men are the same; some seem more manly or masculine than others. The question is, within a sex-role paradigm, how do we make sense of such differences? One fairly common way of accounting for such variations is to suppose that some men may be more thoroughly socialised than others. In other words, it is assumed that they may have gone further in absorbing or assimilating society's lessons on what it means to be a man. However, there are problems with this interpretation. For instance, it lends itself to the idea that the less manly man is a result of some kind of faulty socialisation, and that taking on board the male sex role is necessarily a *good* thing. Of course, there's much to commend in this list of qualities; who would not wish to be strong, dependable and courageous? But what about some of the other things on the list, like dangerous and homophobic? As we heard in Chapter 1, there are those who see the male sex role as something to be resisted, rather than embraced (Pleck and Sawyer, 1974; Nichols, 1975).

Let us return, however, to the issues of the *substance* of masculinity and the associated prospects of change. What does it look like from a sex-role-theory point of view? The first thing to say, perhaps, is that, compared to both the biological and psychoanalytic perspectives, the answer here is much less substantial – in the sense of it being nothing like as deep-seated. Take, for example, Brannon's point about 'no sissy stuff'. There are clear parallels here, of course, with the notion of men's 'flight from the feminine' from Object Relations theory. However, in psychoanalysis, this fear or impulse runs very deep.

Established from an early age, its motivations sit outside of men's consciousness, such that a man may have no real idea why he prefers football to flower-arranging, or news programmes over romantic comedies. Yet in sex-role theory, the masculinisation process is much more 'upfront'. That is, it relies upon an ongoing regime of positive and negative reinforcements, much of which we can see before our very eyes (for example, think about the ways in which boys are often teased). Of course, the idea of being *trained* as a man implies something about men's constitution. The skills of an expert tennis player are *ingrained*, somehow, in their mind and in their muscles. But, as behavioural scientists have shown, such skills must be maintained. So, in (this) theory at least, if society began to encourage men to flutter their eyelashes and don stockings and high heels, it wouldn't be too long before we'd all be following suit.

MASCULINITY – AS POWER

Although sex-role theory retains an enduring influence over the field of masculinity studies, it is not without its critics. Indeed, in the late 1980s, it was subject to a fierce review in a book called *Gender and Power* (Connell, 1987). In the book, Connell exposed a number of serious shortcomings with the sex-role paradigm, amongst the most significant being that it trades on some fundamental ambiguities. On the one hand, Connell said, sex roles are treated as simple *descriptions* of people's character and conduct, with gender *norms* equating to what is seen as normal or typical. Yet, on the other hand, roles are also understood as *prescriptions* or as models for how men (and women) *should* be and behave. Here norms stand not for what is typical or commonplace but for what is *normative* or ideal. Connell argued that if we keep these two meanings apart, then a whole number of interesting questions arise. One is led to ask, for instance, where these standards come from. Who is it that decides what should be seen as 'appropriate' in terms of men's and women's behaviour? We might also want to ponder what might be at stake in those deliberations. What is there to gain through the control of specific gender norms? As far as Connell was concerned, sex-role theory cannot answer these questions, because it lacks any consideration of power. In the hands of sex-role theorists, gender norms are treated as something that is passed down quietly from one generation to the next, like some kind of family heirloom. For Connell, however, the process is much less benign; indeed, it is viewed as a scene of great struggle, upheaval and, at times, even violence.

Without doubt, the best way of appreciating these struggles is to look back in time. Fortunately, in the field of masculinity studies there is no shortage of work dedicated to the illumination of that history (for example, Kimmel, 2012; Tosh, 2005; Arnold and Brady, 2011; Mangan and Walvin, 1987), and what it serves to show is the fluidity of the concept of masculinity. One of the most dramatic illustrations of its mutability comes in the shape of Paul Hoch's (1979) book *White Hero, Black Beast*. Hoch argues that the last three thousand years of Western history has seen a steady oscillation between two basic forms of masculinity: the *puritan* and the *playboy*. The puritan consists of an austere form of masculinity, based around the values of hard work, self-discipline and religious fervour. The playboy, on the other hand, is a hedonist; his life is dedicated to leisure, pleasure and general self-indulgence. For us, though, the crucial issue is what drives these oscillations. Hoch claims that there are, in fact, two different motors. The first is economic necessity. That is, he claims that the reign of the puritan ideal coincides with periods of economic hardship and acts as a stimulus to greater productivity. The more intriguing part of Hoch's analysis is what he sees as at work during times of economic prosperity. In those periods, he says, the definition of masculinity is shaped by the ruling sections of society to both reflect and protect their privileged status. Indeed, Hoch suggests that for most of its long history, the playboy ideal has been an *exclusive* model of masculinity, allowing only the richest and most powerful to qualify (i.e. *as* men).

The history of masculinity is littered with examples of how power is both exercised and sustained by controlling the meaning of what it is to be a man. Consider the right to vote, for instance. Many people are aware that, in countries like the UK, this basic democratic right was for a long time the sole preserve of men – although fewer, perhaps, are aware that, for several centuries, this only applied to the small minority who owned property. In the US, too, women had to wait until the twentieth century before they gained the vote. Before that, the only property requirement placed upon men was that they had ownership of *themselves*. In other words, to vote, they simply needed to be free. But what that meant, of course, was that millions of black men were denied a political voice. Franklin (1993) argues that most black men working on the southern plantations were viewed as subhuman and, as such, were accorded few if any rights. Indeed, he claims that it was only with the Civil Rights movements of the 1960s that black American males were finally accepted as bona fide men. Yet the struggles around gender are by no means always so momentous. For example, Zammuner (1987) conducted a review of some psychological studies of sex-role socialisation. In these studies, children were placed in a playroom full of toys, and the researchers then watched carefully to see how often they selected either gender 'appropriate' or 'inappropriate' objects. A number of patterns emerged. First, they found that most children showed a clear preference for sex-appropriate toys and, second, that these tendencies seem to consolidate as children get older. The other thing they found was that, at every stage, girls made more 'inappropriate' choices than boys (for example, it was more common for a girl to put on the boxing gloves than it was for a boy to pick up a doll). The consensus amongst the researchers was that girls must be more confused about their gender identities. But Zammuner offered a very different interpretation. In her estimations, the girls were displaying *rebelliousness*, not befuddlement. In other words, they were engaged in challenging gender norms, trying to push back the boundaries of what was deemed acceptable or permissible in terms of their own behaviour.

From this perspective, therefore, the key to understanding the nature of masculinity is to see it as *ideological*. Broadly speaking, ideologies are ways of looking at the world – but ways that are always *partial*, in the sense that they work to the advantage of some groups rather than others (Thompson, 1984). For instance, the belief that white people are more civilised than black people was part of a virulent ideology – one which played a crucial role in the expansion of the British Empire and the establishment of the slave trade. Similarly, the suggestion that women are particularly fragile, flighty and irrational can also be seen as ideological, in the way that such views serve to promote and justify their subordination to men. Connell has been a major force in introducing these ideas to masculinity studies, beginning with a paper published a couple of years before *Gender and Power*. 'Towards a New Sociology of Masculinity' (Carrigan *et al.*, 1985) was most notable for launching the concept of *hegemonic masculinity*, which drew directly upon the work of Antonio Gramsci (1971). Gramsci developed the concept of *hegemony* in order to make sense of how the ruling classes maintain their ascendant position in society. Key to his argument was the claim that it worked by gaining others' *consent*, rather than through the exercise of brute force. He also claimed that hegemonic power is never absolute, that ruling ideologies exist in a constant battle or 'war of positions' with other, alternative, ways of understanding the world.

What *hegemonic masculinity* refers to, therefore, is a culturally privileged or exalted way of both thinking about and conducting oneself as a man. According to Connell (1995), it stands not only in contradistinction to femininity but to a range of different masculinities, including gay and black masculinities. Some working in the field equate hegemonic masculinity with the male sex role as described in the previous section. In other words, they see it as a combination of 'qualities', including toughness, courage, ambition and competitiveness. However, this fails to do justice to the subtleties of the concept. Hegemonic masculinity is not a fixed set of traits – and neither is it a particular *type* of man. Its nature is rather more nebulous – and probably best illustrated by way of an (autobiographical) example. As a young boy, I went to a school in a fairly working-class part of town. Without any doubt, the most celebrated boys there were not the ones who excelled in the classroom; they were the ones who were good at football and fighting. There was a clear pecking order. If asked, almost any child (boy or girl) could have reeled off the names of the star performers (in rank order!). I spent my teenage years, however, in a much more middle-class school. In some ways, my early apprenticeship had left me ill equipped to deal with this new environment. I found out very quickly that I couldn't punch my way out of difficult situations. Instead, I had to learn to develop what Peter Redman (Redman and Mac an Ghaill, 1997) called 'intellectual muscularity': that is, the ability to hold one's own through quick-wittedness and a sharp (even caustic) sense of humour. One might ask, then, what does it mean to say that *toughness* and *aggression* are part of hegemonic masculinity? It's not enough to suggest that it encompasses different types of toughness and aggression. The fact is that, in the secondary school, displays of physical violence were seen as unseemly in a gentleman. It spoke of a lack of self-discipline (unless it took place on the rugby field, where it might accrue a certain amount of kudos). As we can see, hegemonic masculinity is complex, context-specific and also, at times, contested.

As mentioned above, Connell (1995) sees hegemonic masculinity as defined in relation to other types of masculinity. Specifically, he talks about there being three alternatives: *subordinate*, *marginalised* and *complicit*. Broadly speaking, subordinate masculinities are those that fly in the face of the hegemonic ideal. The most commonly cited example is that of gay masculinity. It is seen to contravene the dominant form in a number of different ways – the most obvious being, of course, that 'real' men are supposed to sleep with women, not other men! The effete nature of gay masculinity also 'offends' the emphases found in the dominant ideal on the values of ruggedness and restricted emotionality. Marginalised masculinities, on the other hand, involve those cases where men are in some way barred from attaining the hegemonic state. The best examples would include disabled men – marginalised by their reduced vigour and athleticism – but they would also include men from ethnic minorities, denied the opportunities of becoming a 'big wheel' by virtue of systemic racial discrimination. Finally, complicit masculinities describe the situation of, perhaps, most men. As Connell points out, the hegemonic ideal is not one that many men can attain. Nevertheless, most men pay *homage* to it in a variety of ways. Men of all shapes and sizes watch and applaud the physical prowess of sporting superstars, just as many cast admiring glances towards the business tycoons and captains of industry for whom so many of them work. But complicity also operates within the scaled-down world of people's immediate social circles, 'celebrated' in so many minor acts of boasting, besting and bullying.

Feminist theorists have long maintained that power lies at the very heart of what it means to be a man. Indeed, some have gone so far as to suggest that masculinity is, purely and simply, an effect of power (for example, Lips, 1981: Bartky, 1990; see also Radtke and Stam, 1994). For example, men and women have different ways of occupying space. In general, men take up more of it – and not just because they are physically bigger. The fact is that they adopt more expansive postures when sitting or standing, as opposed to women who tend to keep themselves compact (Wex, 1979). Henley (1977) argues that these differences have little to do with anatomy and everything to do with power. In other words, she suggests that if women became the dominant sex, they would spread out more, like men. Some support for this hypothesis can be found in the work of Erving Goffman (1979). He showed that when heterosexual couples hold hands, they do so in a very particular way. Almost always, the back of the man's hand faces forwards. At first sight, it seems like a harmless convention, but in reality it is an act of dominance. Women are perfectly capable of using the same grip, and indeed they do often use it – when holding the hands of *children*.

MASCULINITY – AS PRACTICE

There is a lesson in that last example: whilst masculinity has much to do with ideas or ideologies, it is also about *practice*. A brief scan through just the last couple of paragraphs will serve to highlight a number of different practices relevant to masculinity and the lives of men – from fighting and bullying to playing sport and having sex. When feminists talk about *patriarchy* – or the subordination of women at the hands of men – they are usually invoking a whole range of practices, including domestic abuse, sexual harassment and the imposition of the so-called 'glass ceiling', which restricts the careers of so many women. However, in the last 25 years, there has been a new turn in academics' understandings of the status and significance of gendered practices, which has placed them at the centre of current debates. If we look once again at the vignettes with which this book opened, we should see that they also feature practices of various kinds: displays of control, violence, bluntness/insensitivity and daring. In the eyes of most people – including most social scientists – these practices are just some of the many *symptoms* of masculinity. In other words, they would be seen as manifestations of something that resides somewhere inside the man and makes him what he is. As we have seen earlier in this chapter, academics have spent an awful lot of time and energy trying to figure out or pin down the precise nature of that *thing*. However, in the view of a growing number of academics (and here I would include myself), these efforts seem rather misguided. For us, the kinds of practices described above are not clues about or leads towards the source of masculinity: they *are* the thing itself. All the while our quarry was right under our own noses!

Whilst these arguments are currently in vogue, they draw their inspiration from an older study which provides what I think is, in many ways, an ideal introduction. Harold Garfinkel's (1967) study of Agnes emerged out of hours of interviewing a patient of one of his colleagues at UCLA (the renowned psychiatrist Robert Stoller). Agnes was referred to Stoller because she was seeking a sex-change operation (from male to female) and then, as now, she required a qualified psychiatrist to sign her off for the necessary treatments. Upon first encountering Agnes, Garfinkel found her to be, in almost every respect, a perfectly ordinary young woman. Everything about her appearance and demeanour was feminine. However, Agnes did have a problem: she possessed the genitals of a man. In those interviews, Garfinkel sought to discover for himself the various methods or procedures by which Agnes 'passed' as a ordinary woman. He referred to her as a 'practical methodologist': that is, someone who had developed a deep and detailed understanding of the necessary techniques. Some of those techniques are obvious enough: Agnes had to learn how to dress like a woman, how to apply make-up and how to style her hair. But there were other things that she had to pick up which may not immediately spring to mind. For instance, on one occasion, she found herself amongst a group of women who began exchanging stories about their experiences of the onset of menstruation. Agnes lacked the appropriate biography – but, over time, she soon developed a portfolio of narratives that would see her through such potentially awkward – or even threatening – moments.

Upon hearing about the case of Agnes, it is tempting for us to imagine that she was a very good actress (indeed a 'method' actor, perhaps!). The notion of her attempting to 'pass' as a woman helps to encourage the idea that she was pretending to be something that, in fact, she was not. However, Garfinkel insisted that this was not the case. He didn't dispute that she was acting. Rather, his claim was that *everybody* is acting. The only difference for Agnes (and for other transsexuals) is that, in having to pick up a new set of lines and stage directions, they are made much more conscious of the fact that they are performing. By the time most people reach their teenage years, they have long forgotten the days when they were learning the ropes of how to come across as a normal (enough) boy or girl. Like learning to speak or to ride a bicycle, gender performances soon become *second* nature to us.

In most academic circles today, however, if one speaks about the performance of gender, then the name that springs to most people's lips is not that of Harold Garfinkel but Judith Butler. In her highly acclaimed book *Gender Trouble* (1990), Butler also makes the case that gender is a practical accomplishment – something that we *do*, rather than something that we *are*. Similar to Garfinkel, she looks at extraordinary gender performances as a means highlighting how they are done in ordinary everyday life. Her early focus was on drag artists (drag kings and queens) rather than transsexuals. Superficially (or conventionally), we are likely to understand drag queens as being men who dress up and pretend to be women. But Butler argues that such exaggerated performances (as they often are) serve as a parody of life off-stage. In other words, the obvious artifice involved in the drag queen's enactment of femininity draws critical attention to the status of both his and the audience's everyday performances as authentic men and women.

Compared to Garfinkel, Butler was rather more forthright in claiming that gender is a social or cultural *construction*, rather than something natural. However, by the early 90s, 'constructionist' arguments were becoming far more commonplace (for example, Ortner and Whitehead, 1981; Lorber and Farrell, 1991) – supported, as they were, by a formidable body of theoretical work. One of Butler's major influences was/is the French philosopher Michel Foucault, who is famous for helping to instigate what is often referred to as the 'discursive turn' within the social sciences and humanities. Now, this is certainly not the place to attempt a thoroughgoing account of what this event entailed. It must suffice to say that it revolved around a radical challenge to how we understand the nature of language. At the heart of that challenge was a shift away from seeing it as a system of *representation* and towards a view of language as a form of social *practice*. Think (or look!) back to the account of ideology given earlier in this chapter. I described ideologies as (partial) ways of looking at the world that serve particular interests. This is close (enough) to what Foucault meant by *discourse*. He saw them as constructing the world in particular ways – including, for the likes of Butler, in gendered ways. Butler argued that when a midwife or obstetrician delivers a baby and declares it a boy or a girl (presuming that they can), they aren't simply describing a matter of fact. Rather, she said, they are setting in train a lifelong process whereby the individual is brought into being as a gendered 'subject' through countless, banal invocations. Of course, it's not a case of folk milling around calling out 'it's a boy!' every ten seconds. Rather, it involves an embroilment within a whole regime of discursive practices, including the use of gendered pronouns (he, him, his), gendered names (Peter, Mike, etc.), gendered clothing and so on and so forth – which, taken together, furnish us with a sense of being a normal, natural man (or woman).

It should be clear enough that this view of masculinity as a set of discursive practices constitutes a powerful challenge to our common-sense understandings of what it is to be a man. More than any other approach, perhaps, it serves to unsettle the assumption that gender is something that is natural, inevitable or God-given. It would appear to offer, therefore, unparalleled optimism in terms of the prospects of change. If masculinity is indeed a practical 'accomplishment', it implies that it is something that men can also *decline* to do (Stoltenberg, 1990). It suggests that men can construct themselves differently, leaving behind, perhaps, the more negative or oppressive aspects of their current ways of being. However, it is important to guard against too simplistic a view of the discursive argument. Butler herself has cautioned against seeing gender performances as something with which people can just play around (Butler, 1992). It's not a case, she says, of getting up in the morning and going through one's (discursive) wardrobe trying to decide what gender outfit takes one's fancy. Indeed, there are at least three reasons why this idea is hopelessly naïve. First of all, as Butler points out, the process of gender construction begins from day one (or maybe even earlier, given the prevalence of prenatal ultrasound scanning), which means that the pattern of performances is well established long before the infant can effect any kind of intervention. What this also demonstrates is that gender performances are not solo acts. The construction of masculinities and femininities is a joint or collaborative exercise. As Agnes knew all too well, securing a particular gender always requires the cooperation of others. Finally, one could argue that, just as in case of sex roles, the actual substance of discursive practices is largely a matter of *habit*. Sex-role theorists talk of men *internalising* society's norms and expectations around masculinity. But how is that so different from being 'fluent' in a particular set of discursive activities? Masculinity may not *prompt* men to drink beer or to sit with their legs wide apart, but that's not to say that such acts are not *part* of the man. Indeed, in both of these instances, the symbolic becomes thoroughly embodied.

FURTHER READING

Anderson, E. (2009) *Inclusive Masculinity: The Changing Nature of Masculinities*. London: Routledge.

This book is noteworthy insofar as it offers a critique of Connell's now almost hegemonic concept of hegemonic masculinity. Based on research done in the US and UK, Anderson argues that a new form of masculinity is emerging, prompted by a marked decline in what he calls 'homo-hysteria'.

Carrigan, T., Connell, R.W. and Lee, J. (1985) 'Towards a New Sociology of Masculinity'. *Theory and Society*, 14(5): 551–604.

This was a landmark publication in the development of men and masculinity studies. It offered a devastating critique of the idea of gender socialisation and the male sex role – replacing it with the (now highly influential) concept of hegemonic masculinity.

Halberstam, J. (1998) *Female Masculinity*. London: Duke University Press.

This is an interesting book. In part, it's a work of history, looking at how, over many years, women have assumed aspects of masculine identity. I include it here because of the importance of its central message: that the link between men and masculinity is by no means exclusive.

Reeser, T.W. (2010) *Masculinities in Theory: An Introduction*. Oxford: Blackwell/Wiley.

As evidenced by the title, this volume seeks to foreground matters of theory – and it underlines (very nicely) the point that one can only ever really understand masculinity through theory (even if it comes packaged as 'common sense'). The central theme of the book is about how something so seemingly solid and real (men) is in fact profoundly fluid. Along the way, it considers masculinities in relation to the body, ethnicity and nationhood.

West. C. and Zimmerman, D.H. (1987) 'Doing Gender'. *Gender and Society*, 1(2): 125–51.

Published three years before Judith Butler's acclaimed book *Gender Trouble*, this article sets out, much more clearly than Butler, the case for seeing masculinity (and femininity) as a social performance. These arguments weren't entirely new (Harold Garfinkel's study of 'Agnes' is a better contender for that particular accolade), but we find them here in a condensed and accessible form.

PART 2

3

THE MALE BODY

the body is never outside of history and history never free of
bodily presence

(Connell, 1987: 87)

In Part 1 of this book we spent some time discussing the status of the
male body. As we heard, for many people it exists as the very essence
of what it is to be a man. Masculinity is assumed by them to be an
expression of the body, the playing out of its material design. However, in this chapter we are not going to proceed any further along
these lines. We are not going to pursue those debates about the
impacts of genes, hormones and neural networks. Instead, I want to
use the space to explore the cultural *significance* of the male body – to
examine what it *means* to people, across different times and places.
Along the way, we're going to be touching upon a range of different
themes, including fashion, sport and the experiences of growing old.
Indeed, in the writing of this chapter, I have found it rather difficult
(or artificial) to contain the list of relevant themes. One only has to
think about those topics that make up the second part of this book
to see that, in each and every respect, the bodies of men would
seem to play a prominent role. When I think of the word 'work', for

example, the images that immediately spring to mind are of *manual* labour: the physical practices of digging, lifting and carrying. Of course, for many men these days, work consists of no such thing. For some it might represent a mixture of travel and meetings; for others it will consist of long hours sitting at a desk. But, in almost every case, there is an embodied aspect to these jobs – irrespective of whether it manifests itself as callouses, jet-lag or eye-strain. Fatherhood is equally embodied – from the seminal acts that propel us into fatherhood to the routine physical practices involved in looking after kids. As we will see in Chapter 5, there are some interesting debates about how, if at all, fathering differs from mothering, but no one can dispute the fact that fathers often carry, kiss and cuddle their children, just the same as mothers. The focus of the sixth chapter – on sexuality – is, arguably, the very apotheosis of embodied experience. In the sex lives of most, the body is both the subject and object of erotic activity. It is felt in the aching of desire as well as in the sensual pleasures of touch, taste and smell. Just as tangible are the embodied experiences of violence. As we will see in Chapter 7, violence can take many different forms, from direct physical attacks to acts of emotional abuse. Men's involvement is on both sides of the fence – as perpetrators and victims; but insofar as violence causes injury, deprivation and death, the consequences of violence are invariably physical. Given these multiple connections, it is little wonder that commentators such as Connell (1995), Messner (2005) and Kimmel (1987) claim that the body lies at the heart of what it is to be a man. Yet not everybody concurs. Indeed, in the estimations of writers such as Grosz (1994), Davis, (2002) and Seidler (2000), the status of the male body has never been anything other than marginal. One of the aims of this chapter is to shed some light upon this striking difference of opinion. Another is to demonstrate the pertinence of the quote that sits at the head of the chapter – in showing that the male body is something with a long and interesting history.

FASHIONS OF THE FLESH

From the perspective of the early twenty-first century, it seems strange – perverse even – to suggest that the body is anything other than a core component of modern masculinity. It is not so much, perhaps, the omni-relevance of the male body as its omni-*presence* that makes this suggestion seem so bizarre. In our day-to-day lives it seems as though we are inundated by images of men's bodies – on billboards, magazine covers and television, as well as across all kinds of social media. It doesn't matter whether you are in New York, Tokyo or Sao Paolo: in an era of globalisation, the representations are everywhere – and they seem remarkably consistent, too. The modern male appears as lean and muscular, with clearly defined pectorals and a 'washboard' or 'six-pack' stomach. The idealisation of the **mesomorphic** male (Figure 3.1) is common across the domains of sport (for example, Cristiano Ronaldo), pop music (for example, Justin Bieber), film (for example, Channing Tatum) and fashion. What's more, it can seem as though it has always been thus. As a boy who grew up in the 1970s, I can recall Arnold Schwarzenegger's rise to fame, with the release of the film *Pumping Iron*. Around the same time, newspapers were still running the advertising campaigns of Charles Atlas, in which he invited men to adopt his methods of physical training and to transform themselves from 'puny weaklings' into

Figure 3.1   The idealisation of the mesomorphic male

Source: © Shutterstock/Phil Date.

powerful, 'husky' beefcakes (Reich, 2010). One of the most commonly cited examples of mesomorphic perfection is Michelangelo's statue of *David*, which comes, of course, from much further back in history (the early sixteenth century). Moreover, Michelangelo is said to have taken inspiration from the artistic conventions of the ancient Greeks, who were well known for the valorisation of the (often naked) male body (Goldhill, 2004).

Nevertheless, this impression of historical continuity belies a much more complicated reality. Indeed, whilst the subtitle of Goldhill's book is *How the Ancient World Shapes Our Lives*, at no point did he suggest that things have always remained the same. Of particular relevance here, Goldhill showed how social attitudes towards the male body have fluctuated over time. The ancient Greeks viewed the male body as a symbol of moral and aesthetic virtue. Images of the male body were often used to decorate things like pots, plates and vases. By contrast, women's bodies were regarded as soft, spongy and weak (Aristotle is said to have considered the female body as a kind of deformity!). In the artwork of the ancient Greeks, images of the female form were either absent or hidden away behind a veil of garments. Yet, as Goldhill goes on to explain, at other points in history the disparity was reversed – the display of female flesh became more commonplace, whilst the male body went under wraps. There's a telling story about the occasion when, back in the 1850s, England's Queen Victoria was presented with a plaster-cast replica of Michelangelo's *David*: it is said that she was so taken aback by the sight of David's genitals that a fig leaf was hastily manufactured to mask the offending organs! Of course, these days we like to imagine ourselves as a bit more liberal than our Victorian forebears. We like to think that we live in more enlightened times. But the fact remains that in many parts of the Western world there are still taboos in place around the display of human flesh – particularly in the case of men. In the opening pages of her (excellent) book on the male body, the American academic Susan Bordo reveals how throughout her childhood years, she never once saw her own father naked (Bordo, 1999). Of course, one might conclude that Bordo's father must have been a particularly modest, coy or self-conscious man. However, it is much more likely that the relative invisibility of his body reflected not so much a sense of personal embarrassment or shame but a general lack of concern about the state of men's bodies during that particular period. Writing towards the end of the twentieth century, the distinguished author John Updike said:

> Inhabiting a male body is like having a bank account; as long as it's healthy, you don't think much about it. Compared to the female body, it is a low-maintenance proposition: a shower now and then, trim the fingernails every ten days, a haircut once a month.
>
> (Updike, 1993)

To many people today, such a statement sounds distinctly odd. We are prone to ask: what kind of man cares so little about the state of his own appearance? To the contemporary ear, it smacks of someone who is lazy or complacent. But, again, Updike wasn't being outrageous. Like Bordo's father, he was just a man of his time.

Support for this interpretation can be found in a series of studies conducted by Archer *et al.* (1983). The researchers surveyed the representation of men and women across a wide range of different cultures back to the fifteenth and sixteenth centuries, and they found two clear patterns. First, there were more images of men than of women (by a ratio of 3:2). Men, in this sense, were simply more *visible* than women. More interestingly, their analyses also revealed that there were significant differences in the constitution of those images. Specifically, they found that men were much more likely to be represented by just their heads or faces. In the case of women, more of their bodies were included, not just the head and shoulders. What this seems to imply is that, in both cultural and psychological terms, the body has been more central to our understandings of what it is to be a *woman* than what it is to be a man. I'm not aware of any follow-up studies which have attempted to replicate the work of Archer *et al.*, but, were they to exist, I would be prepared to wager that the results today would be somewhat different. It might well be that there are still significant differences in the ways that men and women are depicted across various forms of media, but I have no doubt that, compared to this 1983 study, the representation of twenty-first-century men would see them as much more *embodied*. Certainly, since the turn of the millennium, there has been a flurry of new studies suggesting not only that men have a strong sense of themselves as embodied, but also that more and more men are dissatisfied with what they see when they look in the mirror (Cohane and Pope, 2001; Tiggermann *et al.*, 2007; Peat *et al.*, 2011). Indeed, there have been several surveys which have suggested that the *majority* of men are now unhappy about aspects of their own physique (although most of this research is based in the U.S – for example, McArdle and Hill, 2009; Pope *et al.*, 2000). Whilst the reported levels of dissatisfaction fall somewhat short of the equivalent statistics for women, in the case of men it seems that this dissatisfaction resolves into two distinctive complaints. Many men these days see themselves as obese, or 'out of shape', and wish that they could lose weight (Monoghan, 2008). However, a significant proportion of men want to become *bigger*, not smaller. They are not looking to become fatter, of course; their desire is to be more muscular. In short, they want to look more like Ronaldo, Bieber and Tatum. Consistent with these rising levels of dissatisfaction is an upsurge in the number of men suffering with various kinds of eating disorder (Hudson *et al.*, 2007; Strother *et al.*, 2012). It wasn't so long ago that **anorexia** and **bulimia** were thought of as problems exclusive to women, but it is now widely recognized that men are also susceptible – albeit, again, in lower numbers. Like many women, men binge, purge and suffer distorted perceptions of their own body image, including a condition peculiar to men (called 'bigorexia') in which sufferers cannot seem to recognise their own (often quite excessive) muscularity, seeing themselves instead as somewhat diminutive or puny.

The question is, therefore, how are we to make sense of these fairly dramatic historical shifts? How can we reconcile the open celebration of the naked male body, as seen in ancient Greece, with the prudishness of the Victorian era in England? With respect to men's own bodies, how can we square the quiet nonchalance (or indifference maybe) displayed by Bordo's father with Cristiano Ronaldo's apparently urgent desire to flaunt his naked torso in front of the viewing eyes of millions? Once again it is tempting is to imagine that, in the case of someone like Ronaldo, it is a matter of personality (i.e. a reflection or consequence of his extroverted and/or narcissistic character) – but insofar as we are dealing here with broad historical *trends*, then an answer cannot be found at the level of individual psychology. The explanation has to stem from the levels of culture and society. If we go back to Goldhill's (2004) account of life in ancient Greece, we find him claiming that, just like today, our ancient forebears would have been under some pressure to keep themselves in good shape. Similar to today, he says, attending the local gymnasium would have been part of their fitness regime. Just as now, they would have been surrounded by advice about the different kinds of diet that would keep them in rude health. However, there is a crucial difference. Goldhill argues that in ancient Greece, it was seen as a man's duty as a citizen to keep himself fit and strong, for a man's body was viewed as the property of the state. Why was the state so invested in the health of its citizenry? It wasn't (like today) in the interests of controlling public spending! Rather, the wider 'logic' was that, so prepared, a citizen was well placed to make a positive contribution to the state in terms of its *defence*. Of all the ancient Greeks, it was the Spartans, of course, who were most renowned for their fighting qualities, but the imperative to remain fit enough for military service would have been felt by every individual male.

There is strong evidence to suggest that this is not the only moment in history in which men's body-consciousness has been raised in the cause of national interests. For instance, during the second half of the nineteenth century, Britain was engaged in a concerted attempt to defend its considerable empire. As an imperial force, its confidence had been shaken by the experiences of both the Crimean (1854–6) and Boer (1899–1902) wars. In particular, the military authorities were shocked by the poor state of health shown by many of those who volunteered for active service. It is no coincidence, therefore, that there emerged around this time a surge of interest in the health and vitality of the British male. Within its public schools, the idea took hold that the character of a man was fashioned more on the playing fields than in the classroom (Mangan, 1986). Particular emphasis was placed upon the importance of team sports, such as cricket and football. As well as cultivating strong and agile bodies, these games taught boys about the values of courage, discipline and fair play. They also encouraged obedience to authority and the ethic of sacrificing oneself for the greater good of the team (read 'nation' – see Dunning, 1986; Kimmel, 1990 and Messner, 2005 for more on the close connections between masculinity, sport and nationhood). Organisations such as the Boys' Brigade (founded in 1883) and the Boy Scouts Movement (1908) also sprang into existence around this time, with their dual emphasis upon religious and military values. In 1880, the author Thomas Hughes published a book entitled *The Manliness of Christ* in which he claimed that Jesus himself was a physically strong and courageous leader. Hughes, of course, was also the author of *Tom Brown's Schooldays* – the eponymous hero of which appeared as a robust and intrepid boy, never afraid to stand up and fight for his own principles. Away from Britain, parallel developments could be seen on the other side of the Atlantic. In the wake of the Civil War (1861–5), the US also witnessed the institutionalisation of team sports (for example, American football, in 1869) and the founding of their own scouting movement (in 1910); and, in place of *Tom Brown's Schooldays,* there was *The Adventures of Tom Sawyer*, written by Mark Twain (first published in 1876).

Nevertheless, to the contemporary eye, the current focus on the male body doesn't appear to be oriented towards those same ideological functions. After all, in the twenty-first century, the military capacities of the modern state do not depend, anything like so much, upon the brawn of the individual soldier. Neither is the body so essential, these days, to the execution of men's work. In the past, a man's physique was often integral to the actual performance of his job. Occupations such as farming, mining and construction work required not just brute strength but also the ability to work long hours in often difficult conditions. However, as we have already noted, in today's economic climate, there is much less call for a strong back and a powerful set of arms. In the current jobs market, good communication and IT skills are more likely to be needed than a decent set of 'abs'. How, then, can we explain the current situation? For writers such as Featherstone (1991) and Shilling (2003), the key to understanding the significance of this latest 'turn' to the body (both male and female) is the culture of **consumerism**. Giddens (1991) argues that, in a consumer society, the body has become a focal point in what he calls people's 'identity projects'. The claim is that the surface of the body has become a medium or platform for communicating *who we are* as individuals. As Pasi Falk (1994) explains, the shape of our bodies and the way that we clothe and adorn them serves as a kind of *text* through which our identities can be interpreted, or *read*. In other words, in contemporary society, our bodies have come to *speak* for us (Davis, 1997; see also Mort, 1988).

Even the most cursory inspection of the covers of magazines such as *Men's Health* or *Men's Fitness* is sufficient to gain a sense of what Falk means by the 'consuming body'. Once again, there is quite a remarkable degree of consistency in terms of their format. The focal point of almost every issue is a photograph of single, mesomorphic male, stripped down to the waist and displaying a finely honed physique. Typically, he will be addressing the camera (and so us as readers) with a steadfast gaze. Arranged around him are the issue's major headlines: 'Rock Hard Abs', 'Strip Away Fat', 'Build Muscle Fast' (sometimes supplemented with the odd line about combating stress or improving one's sex life) – each one encouraging the reader to aspire to the same ideal. What these magazines show us is that there are several different aspects involved in the notion of the body as *consumed*. First of all, there is the obvious sense of the magazine as something to be purchased. Second, there is the *regarding* or taking-in of the images, both on the front cover and inside the magazine. Third, there is the sense of the readers being *themselves* consumed, both in terms of their feelings and anxieties around their own body image and in terms of the various exercise regimes and dietary practices that may follow as a consequence of their engagement with such texts. It is no coincidence that over the course of the last 25 years, male-'grooming' products – including hair gels, moisturisers and facial scrubs – have become a worldwide multi-billion-dollar industry. The rise in demand maps very neatly on to men's growing sense of dissatisfaction with their own bodies (Simpson, 1994). As is so often the case within modern capitalist economies, consumerism doesn't just cater to established needs and desires; it also works to *produce* those needs and desires, in part via the manufacture of discontent.

MALE ANTI-BODIES

What we have seen thus far is that, at various points in history, the bodies of men have been very much at the forefront of society's concerns. We have seen that, during such periods, men have been roused into thinking about and working upon their own bodies – either in the broader interests of national security or, more recently, according to the dictates of consumer culture. However, what is also apparent is that there have been other periods when these pressures simply did not apply. As we saw in the quotation from John Updike, there have been times when men's bodies have been much less at issue – times when, presumably, men could just sit back and relax, comfortable in their own skin. And yet this isn't what Grosz (1994), Davis, (1997) and Seidler (2000) were talking about when they claimed that the body had a marginal status with respect to men and masculinity. What they were referring to was something far more profound. Indeed, what they were suggesting is that, in an important sense, the body is *antithetical* to the very idea of being a man.

All three critics see the origins of this assumption as lodged in the long-standing philosophical traditions of the Western world. According to the likes of René Descartes and John Locke, rationality and logic provided the keys to a true understanding of the world. Emotion, faith and intuition were all seen as much less reliable. Indeed, as Seidler (1989) explains, as irrational phenomena, such things were seen as positively threatening to the expansion of human knowledge. The mind (reason) was privileged over and above the sensations of the body as a guide to what was seen as the truth. Moreover, the body was relegated to something that merely *housed* or contained the mind. As Seidler (1989) also points out, such a view chimed with aspects of Christian orthodoxy, insofar as it placed the mind or spirit on a higher plane than all matters of the flesh (Rutherford, 1988). The body, as something earthly and transient, was seen as something we shared with the rest of the animal kingdom. It was our minds and spirits that set us apart as a different order of being. However, as emphasised by a number of these same authors, the position of the sexes within this cosmology was never entirely symmetrical. More specifically, since the inception of the so-called **Age of Reason**, men have been seen as the more rational half of humanity. For centuries, women were considered ill equipped to contribute to the 'enlightenment project', because they lacked the power of reason. Even today, it is widely felt that men are more rational than women. It is commonly assumed that, compared to men, women understand the world more through emotions and intuitions. And here is the rub: these forms of understanding are seen as somehow issuing from or related to the *body*, rather than the mind (they consist of what the feminist theorist Elizabeth Grosz calls 'corporeal' knowledge – Grosz, 1994). As such, Seidler argues that Western philosophy has left us with a powerful and enormously consequential legacy: a set of symbolic associations that aligns men with the mind, rationality and civilisation – and women, in turn, with the body, emotions and with Nature.

This insight helps to underline the significance of the study, mentioned earlier, by Archer *et al.* (1983). As the authors themselves pointed out, the representation of men in terms of just their heads or faces seems to signify that the essence of a man is what he *thinks* or *knows*, rather than the details of his body. Moreover, as the film critics Laura Mulvey (1975) and Richard Dyer (1993) have pointed out, historically, men have enjoyed the position of being the *subjects*, rather than the *objects*, of the spectatorial gaze. In other words, within that same symbolic complex, men look; they don't expect to be looked at. To be observed, and judged, is the position conventionally occupied by women. I am reminded here of the first time I watched an episode of *Mad Men* (Sky Atlantic): episode 1 of series 5 (I came to the programme late!). In it, the central character, Donald Draper, is sprung a surprise fortieth-birthday party, courtesy of his new wife, Megan. At the end of the evening, after all of the guests have gone home, Don confronts Megan to insist that she never repeats the stunt. Far from grateful, he is deeply angry at having being made the focus of attention. Away from fiction, there are many 'real world' examples that one could draw upon to illustrate the pervasiveness of these same dynamics. For example, Mary Adams (2005) notes the trouble that many dance companies have had in recruiting male performers. She reveals that some dance schools have gone so far as to waive their tuition fees in an attempt to get men through the door. Anyone who knows anything about professional dance will be aware that the physical demands are very high. Stripped off, a male ballet dancer would probably look perfectly 'at home' on the front cover of *Men's Health* magazine. However, the fact that the *raison d'être* of any dance performance is to be a spectacle – where the dancers are there to be looked at and appreciated – puts most men off. Another fascinating illustration comes from Tristan Bridges' **ethnographic** study of gym culture in the US (Bridges, 2009). He describes the tensions and antipathies that existed between two groups of gym-goers: the bodybuilders and the power-lifters. The crux was that power-lifters' training was all about improving their strength, as measured by how much weight they could bench-press or squat. For the bodybuilders, on the other hand, the aims were more aesthetic. Their training methods were designed to make them *look* strong, irrespective of how much weight they could actually lift. Competition, for them, consisted of the *display* of muscle, not in terms of what those muscles could *do* but simply in terms of how they appeared. From the perspective of the power-lifters, this all seemed highly suspect. As one participant explained, real men don't spend half of their time looking in the mirror or 'checking out' other men's bodies.

Except, of course, that some men obviously do! Moreover, the bodybuilders in Bridges' study were not shamed into silence by such taunting. Indeed, they had their own rejoinders. According to them, the power-lifters were a 'bunch of jocks' – which is an interesting designation, insofar as it selects, as a point of critique, the so-called 'dumb machismo' of the power-lifters. One could argue, therefore, that, in effect, the tensions between the two groups of gym-users were based upon or fought around two different 'moments' of masculinity – the older, so-called **retributive** (Chapman and Rutherford, 1988) style of masculinity inhabited by Updike's generation and the more recent **metrosexual** style (Simpson, 1994), as characterized by the likes of Ronaldo, Bieber and Tatum – although, in truth, these moments or styles are not always things that divide one man from another. In other words, as an academic or in everyday life, one cannot just go around placing men into the respective pigeonholes. In reality, we'll find that there can be traces of both styles within a single individual (which is why the notion of *moments* seems so apt). For example, Grogan and Richards (2002) conducted a series of interviews with a range of male participants, aged between eight and twenty-five. One thing they found was that, across the board, body image was seen as important for their participants, and there was a strong consensus, too, that the muscular, or mesomorphic, body was the one that they saw as ideal. Nevertheless, there were tensions within the accounts of their interviewees; whilst they claimed that they wanted to be muscly, they insisted that they didn't want to be *too* muscly. Bodybuilders were seen as overly concerned or 'obsessed' with how they looked. Grogan and Richards's interviewees trod a delicate path between presenting themselves as bothered – but not too bothered – about their physical appearances. Having a 'fit' body was taken as a positive sign of good discipline and self-respect, but, at the same time, too many hours spent at the gym (or looking at oneself in the mirror) smacked of caring too much about the opinions of others, of not 'being your own man'. Similar patterns of accounting were also seen in a later study by Gill *et al.* (2005), but they also pointed out that, in describing their own body regimes or practices, their interviewees framed everything in terms of health and fitness. Wanting to look good just for the sake of looking good was widely disavowed. Where vanity or narcissism was acknowledged at all, it was always in *other* men, never in themselves.

IN-DIFFERENT BODIES

Like Grogan and Richards (2002), the research of Gill *et al.* (2005) focused on the sense-making of young men. In a way, it was an obvious choice, given that this latest 'turn to the body' (Shilling, 2003) seems to have taken so much more concerted a hold amongst the younger sections of society. Gill *et al.* note that, in the course of no more than a decade, 'men's bodies *as bodies* have gone from near invisibility to hypervisibility' (39), but what we are actually *seeing* is men from a fairly narrow age range – from teens through to their early thirties (Thompson, 2006). Interestingly, Calasanti and King (2005) claim that Masculinity Studies shares a similar bias; within that literature, older men are relatively hard to spot. Thompson (1994) would concur; in his view, gerontology has more to say about this particular demographic group – but even here, he claims, the view is restricted. He argues that gerontology looks at old men in terms of their *age*, not their gender. So, once again, older men as *men* get ignored. There is probably quite a strong link between the absence of older men in popular/visual culture and in Masculinity Studies. Put very simply, if masculinity is widely thought of as a matter of embodiment – if it is being equated more and more with things like strength, vigour and athleticism – then, as they get older, it becomes increasingly difficult for men to register or count as men (Thompson, 1994; Sandberg, 2011). Of course, insofar as today's old men, like

Updike, still see matters of the body as peripheral to their sense of gendered self, they may be somewhat inoculated against these cultural developments. Indeed, that might help to explain why, in Peat *et al.* (2011), it was actually *younger* men who felt most unhappy with their bodies (despite being in somewhat better shape). However, as the 'cult of the body' continues to displace those 'old fashioned' views, one would expect to see a significant rise in the proportion of men who greet middle age feeling profoundly unsettled by the loss of hair, muscle mass and skin tone.

Searching through the literature, one area where we do find a bit more attention paid to the issue of the ageing body is in relation to the experiences of gay men. Over the years, a number of theorists have claimed that gay culture places a greater emphasis on the aesthetics of the body compared to the heterosexual realm (for example, Atkins, 1998; Levesque and Vichesky, 2006; Morrison *et al.*, 2004). There is certainly some evidence to suggest that gay men are more likely than straight men to feel dissatisfied with their own bodies (McArdle and Hill, 2009; Tiggermann *et al.*, 2007). One line of explanation for these differences is that within gay culture, the regulation of the gaze is quite unlike how it is in straight society. Here the body of the man is very much the object of others' attention. The gay man understands very well that he will be looked at – just as he looks at others – and, as a consequence, his sense of his own physical appearance will loom larger in his consciousness than would be the case for the average heterosexual man. This would also help to account for why gay men seem to feel middle-aged or old ahead of their heterosexual counterparts (Jones and Pugh, 2005; Slevin and Linneman, 2010). All that said, there are signs that the gap between gay and straight sensibilities around the body may be closing – and fast – particularly with regards to levels of satisfaction. It is not a very 'happy' trend, in that the convergence seems to emerge out of a sharp rise in the extent to which *all* men feel dissatisfied with the size and shape of their bodies. In McArdle and Hill's (2009) study, for example, more than 90 per cent of their participants admitted that they would like to be either slimmer or more muscly (or both).

In the course of her discussions around the male body, Bordo (1999) suggests that gay culture has been a driving influence in mainstream society's turn towards the body. Citing Gaines and Churcher's (1994) biography of Calvin Klein, she describes how the designer's familiarity with the New York gay scene inspired him to play around with the cut of traditional jeans, so that they hugged the contours of the wearer's body. By shortening the 'rise' of the trousers (i.e. the distance between the waistband and the crotch) he was able to accentuate both the shape of the wearer's buttocks and, in the case of men, the pouch containing his genitals. The jeans were an instant hit – and, of course, not just amongst the gay community. The style soon became the standard cut and, along with underwear, shirts and T-shirts, body-hugging garments became staples of the high street. Today, millions of men wander around dressed in such a way that showcases and sexualises their own body. Few would suspect that, in doing so, they are continuing the legacy of gay culture.

One of the surest indicators of the significance of the body in relation to men and masculinity is the fact that physical disability seems to have a gendered dimension. Writing about his own experiences of living with a serious spinal condition, Murphy (1987) echoes the point made by Thompson (1994): that when masculinity is associated with the attributes of strength and vitality, it can be challenging for disabled men to conform to the standard definitions of manliness. Even more than in the case of the elderly, the image of the physically disabled man is conspicuously absent from mainstream culture. Rarely do we see the amputee, the blind man or the wheelchair-bound on our screens, phones and tablets; neither do such images spring to mind when we think of the archetypal man. However, as Shuttleworth et al. (2012) point out, it is a mistake to treat disability as a unitary phenomenon. Even if we restrict our attention to physical disabilities, the issues are tremendously varied (for example, from deafness to full quadriplegia), and they impact on gender in a variety of ways. The authors also draw an important distinction between those men who are born with disabilities and those that incur them at some point during their lives. The experiences of those men whose identities are interrupted by injury or chronic illness and those who have never known anything else can be quite different. Moreover, as Watson (1998) makes clear, the disabled shouldn't be thought of as passive victims. Some disabled men might accept a diminished sense of their own masculinity, but others have found ways to work around their disability – either by developing compensatory strategies (for example, taking up a sport for the disabled, such as wheelchair basketball; see Valentine, 1999) or by questioning the very ideology which serves to marginalise disabled men (Gerschick and Miller, 1995; Shakespeare, 1999).

'MASCELLANY'

We could easily go on, in this chapter, to consider other forms of difference. We could look at the black body, working-class bodies, the transsexual body; all of these are important topics which, given the space, could extend and enrich our understanding. However, I would like to dedicate what little space remains for this chapter to the consideration of two topics which provide interesting links between the issues of embodiment and masculinity. The first of these is sport. I've touched upon sport a few times already in this chapter, and it will emerge again, as a theme, later on in the book. But it is worth stressing here the role that sport has played, and continues to play, in the regulation of the male body. It's easy to imagine that sport is just a matter of fun and games, but, as Messner (2005) makes clear, it is an institution which helps both to create and maintain masculinity. In schools all over the Western world, sports have been organised along gendered lines – and usually with more options for boys (rugby, football, baseball, basketball, etc.). There is nothing arbitrary about these divisions: most boy's/men's sports have at some point been deemed unsuitable for girls/women, often on account of the fact that they involve a level of aggression and violent contact that was seen as either unbecoming of women or beyond their very nature. But in Messner's view, such thinking puts the cart before the horse. In a fascinating essay, Iris Marion Young (2005) writes about how boys learn to use their whole bodies when they throw, whereas girls tend to use just their lower arms. She notes that, in attempts to catch, a boy will tend to move towards the object, to intercept it in its flight, whereas girls will often see the ball as coming *at* them and so cower, duck or run away. Young claims that sport teaches boys to move around in the world, to utilise space and to use their bodies to *do* things, whereas girls learn to restrict their movements and to see their bodies as a limitation on what they might achieve. They experience their bodies as something fragile, vulnerable and unreliable. There's a lovely passage, too, in a book by David Jackson, where he describes the formative nature of these sporting routines. He writes:

> All through my childhood I hardened my body through everyday sporting practice . . . I used to dribble a balding tennis ball along the pavement all the one and a half miles to school, learning to play wall-passes, selling dummies to lamp-posts, or sending the ball round one way and going the other way with my body. Then at primary school and later at grammar school I used to join in the rushing melee of playing football in boys-only yards, rarely connecting with the ball but hacking, lunging and swiping at it as it whizzed past. In the evenings I used to spend solitary hours kicking a ball against a garage door and learning to trap the rebound, bring the ball down under control and send it back against the door or a neighbouring brick wall . . . Thrusting for goal over the years has shaped my body in a particular way . . . The clenched legacies of my past determination to win or achieve or score are there in the rigid way I tense and hold my body.
>
> (Jackson, 1990: 207, 220)

This *disciplining* of the body has its delights and detractions. On the plus side, it leaves the body fit, strong and capable. The sense of *mastery* involved in playing sport can be a source of profound enjoyment. On the other hand, organised sports often encourage men to suffer pain and, sometimes, to inflict it upon others. In many professional sports, playing whilst compromised by injury is not only common-place but expected (Curry, 1993). Of course, in the twenty-first century, sport as a 'male preserve' (Dunning, 1986) is under con-siderable pressure. Women now play professional cricket, rugby and football (soccer); they can win Olympic medals in boxing, the marathon and the pole vault (although not the decathlon – women still do the seven-event heptathlon). In most cases, women have had to fight hard to be allowed to compete. For years, they were disqualified on the grounds that, for them, such activities were unseemly and unsafe. But what was really being defended was not women's well-being so much as the opportunity for men to feel a sense of positive difference (and superiority).

There's a potential link here with the second and final topic. Whilst the conspicuous display of male flesh may have been witnessed at other points in the past, this latest turn does appear to have some rather novel features – one of which is the prevalence of *tattoos*. Tattoos are by no means a twenty-first-century development, of course. As Pasi Falk (1995) explains, people have been marking their own and others' flesh for thousands of years. However, in the last couple of decades tattoos seem to have become much more commonplace (Sweetman, 1999). David Beckham (Figure 3.2) is famous for his tattoos as well as his sporting prowess. Apparently, he has over thirty tattoos, distributed mainly across his arms, chest and back. Many rugby players, cricketers and boxers have followed suit in having

Figure 3.2   David Beckham

Source: © Photo Works/Shutterstock.com.

entire limbs (or more) covered with tattoos, as have film, television and music performers. What is going on? How are we to understand this recent trend? According to Shilling (2003), the answer lies in the shift to consumer culture and the rendering of the body as an identity project (Giddens, 1991). Paul Sweetman (1999) conducted a series of interviews in which he spoke to people about their motivations for having a tattoo. One of the most common refrains was that they had them 'just to be a bit different' – which seems rather ironic given their recent popularity. But Sweetman argues that, for many of his interviewees, the decision to have a tattoo was not taken lightly. He reports that they often invested considerable time and thought in the particular image or design. As in Beckham's case, many of the tattoos carried some personal significance: the names of loved ones, favourite mottos, epithets and symbols. The more abstract designs were also selected or created as a means of *self-expression*. Sweetman argues that, far from being just 'trendy', these inscriptions could be thought of as a fight *against* fashion. Some of his interviewees spoke about the significance of having something permanently written in the flesh (Falk, 1995). For Sweetman, the tattoos were serving to stabilise or 'anchor' people's identities in a time of dizzying cultural change.

As compelling as these arguments are, I would argue that there is also a gendered dimension to these practices of inscribing the flesh. Sweetman recognises that a tattoo can function as a sign of commitment, paid for not just in terms of the permanence of the marking but in terms of the *pain* endured in its establishment. Getting a tattoo is at the very least an uncomfortable experience; therefore, getting a large tattoo or a lot of them together adds up to good deal of pain. What this means is that tattoos are a symbol not just of commitment but of *physical endurance* – one of the keynotes of hegemonic masculinity. Of course, as with modern sport, tattoos are not a male preserve; plenty of women have them, including Victoria Beckham. However, in general, women's tattooing is lighter and more discreet – and often avoids the most painful parts of the body, such as the head, elbows and ribcage. In procuring a full-arm or 'sleeve' tattoo, men may well be aiming 'just to be a bit different'; but the point of distinction is more likely to be women as it is other men.

FURTHER READING

Dyer, R. (2002) 'The White Man's Muscles'. In R. Adams and D. Savran (eds) *The Masculinity Reader*. Oxford: Blackwell (pp. 262–73).
This is a short but interesting analysis of the relationship between 'race' and the male body (from what, within academic circles, is called a *post-colonial* perspective).

Edwards, T. (1997) *Men in the Mirror: Men's Fashion, Masculinity and Consumer Society*. London: Cassell.
This book examines not the male body so much as its adornment in terms of clothes and fashion. Edwards looks at the concept of the New Man and the role of men's magazines in drawing men deep into consumer culture.

Fine, C. (2010) *Delusions of Gender: How Our Minds, Society, and Neurosexism Create Difference*. London: Icon Books.
Neuroscience is a force to be reckoned with in the current academic (and political) climate – but Fine takes a critical look at some of its claims around gender. The work is authoritative, incisive and, at times, really funny.

Gill, R., Henwood, K. and McLean, C. (2005) 'Body Projects and the Regulation of Normative Masculinity'. *Body and Society*, 11(1): 37–62.
This is a fascinating article which looks at how men attempt to reconcile a (post)modern interest in their own and other men's bodies and the older idea that men aren't interested in matters of appearance.

Young, I.M. (2005) 'Throwing like a Girl: A phenomenology of feminine body comportment, motility, and spatiality'. In *On Female Body Experience: 'Throwing like a Girl' and Other Essays*. Oxford: Oxford University Press (pp. 27–45).
Primarily focused on the physicality of women and girls, as a counterpoint, this essay contains tremendous insights into how men and boys occupy space in the course of everyday life.

MEN AND WORK

I recall sitting in a physics lesson at school and hearing that, within that discipline, *work* could be defined as 'force multiplied by distance'. Almost all of the other formulae have long since faded from memory – but not that one, as it seems to me to capture the very essence of work. When, as a boy, the coal was delivered to our family home and the men shuttled back and forth from lorry to outhouse carrying heavy sacks of fuel, that *looked* to me like work – force over distance – and yet, as I pointed out in the previous chapter, *manual* labour is by no means the only thing that qualifies as work. Indeed, one of the issues that we'll be examining in this chapter will be the shifting nature of work – away from what might be thought of as *heavy* industry and towards more sedentary, intellectually based endeavours. Nevertheless, I would argue that it is still useful to think about why manual labour appears to be work *par excellence*, for I think that it opens the door to our seeing the very close connections that exist between work and masculinity.

I would like to start our exploration by relating another memory that derives from those early years. It involves being asked if my mother worked. 'No,' I replied, 'she doesn't work. She's just a housewife.' Such a response is revealing in several ways. First of all, it shows us that, in the past at least, not all labour *counts* as work.

Housework involves plenty of 'graft': scrubbing and cleaning, pegging out the laundry, carrying home heavy bags of groceries – but to me, back then, work meant *paid* employment, not 'voluntary' domestic labour. In my young eyes, people went *out* to work; it took place in the public sphere, not in the confines of the home. My naïve response also reveals a clear hierarchy between those different spheres of operation. Note that my mother was 'just' a housewife; all of her cooking, cleaning and taking (very good) care of me was diminished in terms of its perceived value. It was my father, as the breadwinner, who stood out and was celebrated as the worker in our household. Of course, I was by no means alone in looking at the world in those ways; in fact, at the time, my perspective was pretty much common sense. But, like so many of these things, it was a way of looking that had a specific history.

There is some speculation amongst historians about when the signs first appeared of a gendered division of labour. Cynthia Cockburn (1985) argues that there is evidence of a split dating back many thousands of years, to the beginning of the Bronze Age. But, like most of her peers, she maintains that the sharpest divide has emerged quite recently – since the start of the Industrial Revolution. In **agrarian societies** it was (and still is) quite common for men and women to work side by side and, before industrialisation, there was little or no separation between the realms of work and home. Within the UK, it was only with the emergence of the first factories, mines and mills that people began to *go out* to work – and initially, at least, both sexes were involved. Many people today are surprised to hear that, during the early nineteenth century, women (and indeed children) were a common sight in many mines and factories. But, as time wore on, women were gradually excluded from these 'primary' or heavy industries and ushered instead into areas of the economy that we still see today as female-dominated – for example, school teaching, dress-making and nursing (Hall, 1992; Walby, 2009). Of course the Industrial Revolution did much more than just put space between work and home; for many it also resulted in the *movement* of home – from rural areas into the rapidly expanding urban centres. The concentration of the new industrial working classes had its own effects, not least the formation of the first trade unions. Together, they succeeded in raising the wage levels of workers, particularly in the more highly skilled trades such as cabinet and toolmaking (Cockburn, 1985). However, to the extent that women were excluded from such trades, it meant that, within many working-class households, the man's wages exceeded those of the woman. In other words, *he* became the major breadwinner. Moreover, as Hall (1992) points out, during the nineteenth century, the concept of the 'family wage' made its first appearance (in England). This constituted an order of money seen as sufficient to support not just the individual worker but their whole family unit. Within that particular echelon of the workforce (i.e. skilled labour or tradesmen) it became not only possible for a man to support his wife and children financially but a matter of personal pride and respectability that he did so. This was certainly the case with my own family. It was no coincidence that my mother 'gave up work' when she married my father and embarked on having children. It was expected. Had she continued with her secretarial role – had she sought to become a 'working mum' – it would have been very much frowned upon – and the force of that disapproval would have been felt as much by my father as by her.

THE GENDERING OF WORK

As circumstances would have it, the 1950s in the UK were something of a tipping point in terms of the disparities between men's and women's involvement in paid employment. As numerous historians have pointed out, at the end of the Second World War, considerable pressure was put upon women to relinquish their positions within the economy in order to make way for the men returning home. In various ways (some subtle, others much less so) it was implied that a woman's place was in the home – and given that, by the midpoint of the twentieth century, only one in five married women were in gainful employment (Cohen, 1988), it would appear that the campaign was largely successful. What this meant was that, to a significant degree, being in paid employment became a *mark* of masculinity (Haywood and Mac an Ghaill, 2003). Being a man meant being the *provider*, the person whose wages funded the lives of his *dependents*. Various authors have written about the symbolic importance for men of being employed. One of the best illustrations comes in the form of Paul Willis's classic ethnography, *Learning to Labour* (Willis, 1977), in which he describes how working-class boys looked forward to or anticipated leaving school and getting a job – almost as a rite of passage. To them, having a job meant freedom and independence; in short, it meant being a man and no longer a boy. Likewise, Andrew Tolson (1977) wrote about how the role of the breadwinner helped to secure men's power and authority within the family unit. He described the way that, amongst many working-class families, the father's arrival home from work saw him treated like a VIP. His dinner would be ready for him on the table the moment he walked in; a bath would be drawn for him so that he could wash away the dust and dirt accumulated from a day spent in the factory, field or mine. Tolson argued that, given such circumstances, it was little wonder that boys looked forward so avidly to joining the ranks of working men. There was something *heroic* about the role of the breadwinner – which was particularly evident in those jobs that were especially dirty, dangerous and physically demanding. There, more than anywhere, one could see his labour as an act of dutiful self-sacrifice.

Of course, since the publication of these two books, the nature of the economic landscape in the UK (and elsewhere) has changed beyond all recognition. From the late 1970s onwards, many countries in the developed world have seen a sharp decline in the kinds of industry that, in the past, have served to underpin and sustain men's privileged status within their own families. In both the UK and the US, for example, the number of jobs in manufacturing has plummeted over the last 40 years, leaving entire regions in a state of chronic decline and decay (for example, the US 'rust belt', located in the north-east, taking in cities such as Pittsburgh, Cleveland and Detroit). These dramatic developments can be seen as one of the consequences of *globalisation*. Here is certainly not the place to attempt a detailed examination of this highly complex concept (see Steger, 2013 and Scholte, 2005 for short introductions); however, I do want to pick up on one of its key themes. Globalisation involves the worldwide spread of so-called *neo-liberalist* ideology (Harvey, 2005), which holds as sacrosanct the importance of 'free trade' relations within a global market system. Under these conditions, countries are discouraged or even debarred from protecting their own internal economies by measures such as high import tariffs. In the UK, state subsidies of key industries like coal, steel and car manufacture were stopped for being 'anti-competitive'. So, today, the UK imports most of its coal from Russia, whilst almost all of its own mines lie abandoned and derelict. It is cheaper to import foreign coal, not least because Russian miners work for less than half the wages of their UK counterparts.

The effects of globalisation have resulted in a major shake-up across many parts of the world, both in terms of the nature of work and the constitution of those employed. Some of the fastest growing economies include countries such as India, China and Kenya – which all have vast supplies of labour. In no small part, the expansion of these economies has been fuelled by foreign investment from the West. Many large multinational companies have taken advantage of those reserves of cheap labour for the outsourcing of their production lines. Indeed, the drive to maximise profits sees plenty of companies seeking out the very lowest rates of pay (as little as 18 cents or 12 pence per hour), which often involves the employment of women (Gap, Benetton, Nike and, more recently, Primark, are just some of the companies that have been accused of using 'sweatshop' labour in countries like India and Bangladesh – see the Rana Plaza disaster of April 2013). In many Western countries, the number of women in paid employment has also been on the rise, again because they tend to be cheaper. This is not to suggest, of course, that the world of work is no longer dominated by men. A recent United Nations Development Report (2014) showed that in almost every country around the globe, there are more men than women in paid employment. But the point is that the order of discrepancy varies considerably from place to place. Some of the most equitable arrangements are to be found in Africa (for example, Rwanda, Malawi and Burundi) and the Nordic countries of Norway, Sweden and Iceland. At the other end of the scale, the biggest margins are reserved for the Arab states of Algeria, Iran and Saudi Arabia (where the ratio of men to women is around five to one). Most of Western Europe and North America hovers around the 80–5 per cent level (i.e. around four women employed for every five men). What this seems to show is that in places like the UK, the realm of paid employment is far less gendered now than it was in the middle part of the twentieth century.

However, the gendering of work is not just a matter of who is in receipt of wages for their labours. As I mentioned earlier, it has often been the case that where women have been in paid employment, they have been doing different kinds of job than men. Many of those jobs fall under the four Cs of cleaning, caring, clerical work and catering, whereas men have traditionally dominated the fields of science and engineering, politics, the armed forces, construction work, law . . . (it's a long list). There are areas of the economy where the balance is much more equal and yet, even there, one has to be careful not to be too hasty in concluding that the playing field is now level. The education sector in the UK serves as a useful case in point. In 2010, around 13 per cent of UK primary-school teachers were male; at secondary-school level, the figure stood at 37 per cent (Department of Education, 2011). Students attending colleges of further education would have found that 45 per cent of their teachers were men, whereas at university, the majority (55 per cent) of lecturers were male. It is clear that there is a close correlation between the level of education and the extent of men's involvement (some would argue that men's enthusiasm wanes the more that the work resembles childcare!). In other words, the *distribution* of men and women within the sector is highly asymmetrical. And there's more . . . as we've just heard, in the UK's secondary schools, most of the teachers are women; and yet 64 per cent of the head teachers are male. Likewise, of the 150 universities in the UK, nearly 90 per cent are led by a male vice-chancellor. In other words, the further up the hierarchy one goes, the greater the concentration of men. Education is by no means unusual in this patterning. As I write, just 5 per cent of CEOs in the FTSE 100 are women, and over 90 per cent of UK company directors are male. And the same can be said for so many other countries dotted around the globe. Figure 4.1 was taken in 2012 and features a gathering of European heads of state. At a glance, one can see that it is dominated by men.

This is the reality which has prompted feminists to claim that we live in a 'man's world'. One looks around and sees that men occupy most of the key positions in public life, most of the jobs that carry with them real power, authority – and money. Ironically, this advantage was never so conspicuous back in the 1950s, even though the margins back then were still greater. As breadwinners, men were seen to be assuming those positions *on behalf* of their families. Within the framework of the 'two spheres' (i.e. public and private), men

Figure 4.1 European heads of state

Source: © Drop of Light/Shutterstock.com.

weren't viewed as being in competition with their wives; rather, work was seen as something men did in holding up their half of the bargain. He worked to put a roof over her head and food on the table; she, in return, took care to ensure that when he came home from work, the house was tidy and the table was set. It was only as the century wore on, and as women emerged from the confines of the home to become keen competitors in the new jobs market, that men's continued occupation of those same key positions took on a rather different complexion. In countries like the UK, equal-rights legislation was brought into effect around the practices of hiring, firing and offering promotions, making it illegal for organisations to discriminate against a person on the grounds of their sex – and yet the gender gap persists. Indeed, as Stephen Whitehead put it:

> The fact of whether you are a man or a woman will have a direct bearing on your chances of becoming, for example, a company director, politician, surgeon, senior manager, army officer, detective, professional athlete, priest, judge, high-ranking civil servant, economist, professor and so on . . . Also, if you are a woman in paid employment, you are more likely than a man to be in temporary, non-unionized, part-time, low-skilled, lower-paid work.
>
> (Whitehead, 2002: 39)

All of the evidence points, he says, to the fact that women still suffer a 'female forfeit' in terms of the rewards that they can expect work to bring them over the course of their adult lives.

How can we explain this situation? To paraphrase Whitehead, how can material advantage, autonomy and opportunity remain gendered, despite the concerted efforts of political campaigners, liberal administrations and concrete legislative action? As ever, there are no easy answers to such a question. Some would no doubt argue that it reflects men's keener competitive edge – that it derives from their greater ambitions and ruthless determination to succeed. Others would contend that the gap remains simply on account of the fact that those who are in power (i.e. men) have little or no interest in relinquishing their advantage – that it suits men very well to maintain a culture of defending 'jobs for the boys'. But neither of these arguments will do. The first explanation fails to acknowledge that, over the years, social scientists have found it virtually impossible to demonstrate that there are, in fact, generalisable differences between men and women in terms of competitiveness and ambition (or indeed any other psychological traits or characteristics), despite an enormous effort (see Maccoby and Jacklin, 1974; Segal, 2007 for reviews). The second argument suffers not only from being conspiratorial but implying that women are hapless victims, powerless to do anything about the circumstances in which they live. Feminists have tried very hard to dispel this notion. For example, Sylvia Walby (1990) claims that Western history is marked by the positive interventions of women, not least in the form of the anti-sex-discrimination laws that we find in so many parts of the developed world. Men's privileged position with respect to the world of work continues in spite of those efforts, held in place by a combination of factors which require closer and more subtle analysis. What is more, in looking towards those factors, we will begin to see whole new ways of thinking about the gendering of work.

GENDERED INSTITUTIONS

One of the most intriguing and compelling explanations of men's continued advantage in the world of work is that, more than women, men fit the contours and culture of organisational life. One of the earliest advocates of this position was the feminist sociologist Joan Acker. In a landmark piece (Acker, 1990), she suggested that, as well as human beings, organisations could be gendered. She claimed that most modern institutions have built into them an implicit model of the ideal worker, as someone who is rational, analytical and tough-minded. As others have pointed out (Bem, 1974; Brannon, 1976), all of these qualities are ones that are firmly associated with men and masculinity. She argued that, for most organisations, the ideal employee is somebody who will be utterly dedicated to their work, a person who, as they say, 'lives and breathes' the firm or corporation. Again, she said, this privileges men – as it takes little or no account of people's other life commitments, such as to one's family. Organisations may well look favourably upon the employee who gets into work at 8am and stays until well after 7pm, but, as Acker and others have since pointed out (Pateman, 1988; Wajcman, 1998), this sits very uncomfortably with those who have to make their children's breakfast, take them to school and then pick them up again afterwards. Acker also looked at how organisations went about the process of job evaluation. This is where companies attempt to identify the specific demands that are made by a particular position or role – against which pay levels are then set. What she found was that companies privileged certain kinds of work over others on what she saw as being the most arbitrary of bases. For example, she found that they routinely judged working with money as carrying greater responsibilities and demanding higher levels of skill compared to working with people. Why should the starting salary of someone bound for the finance office exceed that set for a person beginning their career in human resources (HR)? Similar to Cockburn (1985), Acker came to the conclusion that the 'logic' was simply this: if it is a job that is mainly done by women, then it can't be all that demanding!

As we have just heard, all around the globe, women find it harder to make it into senior positions within organisations. One might imagine that managing others would fall very neatly into women's (presumed) skill set; and yet, as Collinson and Hearn (1996) explain, the very concept of management can be seen as being inscribed within masculinist terms. They point out that the roots of the word stem from a sixteenth-century Italian term ('menagerie') meaning to direct and control – especially within the context of war. This theme is further developed in Judy Wajcman's book *Managing like a Man* (Wajcman, 1998), where she explains how, in spite of the prevalence of equal-opportunities policies and rhetoric, corporations still frame their expectations for managers within a solidly masculine mould. In their eyes, the ideal manager is someone who is decisive, strategic and dispassionate. An effective manager will recognise what needs to be done, get on with doing it and won't lose too much sleep about who might get hurt along the way. Such a disregard for people's feelings is a hallmark of modern masculinity (look again at the exchange between Tiger and Ehrenreich at the start of Chapter 1). Moreover, as Wajcman (1998) explains, when men behave in such a highly instrumental manner, they are typically admired, commended and rewarded for being a good manager; but when women do the same, they often meet with a very different kind of reaction. Strong and assertive female managers are often perceived as aggressive and overbearing. In effect, women managers find themselves in a no-win situation. If they try to fit in with the prevailing (masculine) culture, they are likely to find themselves unpopular at work – and, hence, not the right candidate for promotion. On the other hand, if they eschew that culture and manage in ways that utilise a 'softer' skill set, then they also stand to miss out, on account of not being seen to 'have what it takes'. Wajcman shows that there are other implications that stem from the way that organisations read the actions of male and female managers through a conventional gender 'lens'. She points out that when male employees marry, this is often seen as good for the corporation, insofar as it is thought to bind him even more closely to his work, as a means of fulfilling his duties as provider to his new family. But when a female employee marries, this is often seen in negative terms. Instead of tying her to the company, her marriage is seen to herald the loosening of her commitment. It's commonly assumed (implicitly at least) that her priorities will shift away from work and towards the domestic sphere, in support of her new husband.

Over the years, there have been some fascinating analyses produced within the field of sociology which look at men's particular engagement with work. Theorists have noted that men's sense of self is often very firmly bound up with the work that they do and, relatedly, that unemployment tends to hit men harder than is generally the case for women (Willott and Griffin, 1997). One of the most notable and often quoted sources is Sally Hacker's book *Pleasure, Power and Technology* (Hacker, 1989), in which she explores the relationship between men and technology. Hacker based her analysis on a period of fieldwork at MIT (Massachusetts Institute of Technology) amongst a cohort of engineering students. To some extent, the picture she painted of these young men was as a rather 'geeky' group. She noted that many of them led somewhat solitary lives, preferring to spend their time thinking about engineering problems rather than cultivating friendships. It is a story that chimes with the research conducted a few years earlier by Cynthia Cockburn (1985). Some of the men she interviewed claimed that they would gladly accept a reduced level of income if it meant being able to work on the most complex technological problems. What mattered to them most was the intellectual and practical *challenge* posed by their work. In their responses, Cockburn heard echoes of one of the founding fathers of modern science, Francis Bacon, who spoke about trying to 'penetrate Nature's secrets' and 'storming her castles'. Interestingly, Hacker also claimed to have detected a certain 'eroticisation' of technology – that is, deep sexual undertones – in the way that her respondents spoke about their work as engineers. As we heard in Chapter 2, Freud thought that men's investment in science (and many other cultural activities) could be seen as a form of 'sublimation', a way of channelling forbidden sexual desires and fantasies into safer, more socially acceptable, avenues. Likewise, authors such as Hacker (1989), Seidler (1989) and Kerfoot and Knights (1996) claim that men's efforts to conquer and control nature (through science and technology) is largely fuelled by underlying or unconscious anxieties around their own (unruly) sexuality. In their eyes, dedicating oneself to working on complex technological problems is not just a useful distraction: it also offers men some level of reassurance that they still have control of the reins – that they can still direct events and impose their will upon the world.

There are some writers in the field of masculinity studies who would want to maintain that whilst men's strong identification with work is by no means new, it has reached new heights under the rise of neo-liberalism. Once again, Connell has been at the forefront of these claims (Connell, 1995; Connell and Wood, 2005). We hear a lot these days about 'enterprise culture'. Many of those EU leaders in Figure 4.1 would see one of their main political aims as promoting a spirit of entrepreneurialism – encouraging the citizens of their respective countries to create wealth and jobs through the setting up of their own businesses. Many schools and universities (including my own institution) see the development of entrepreneurial skills as a key part of their remit. As Miller and Rose (1990) explain, in an enterprise culture, work is framed not as a necessary encumbrance but as an opportunity to flourish as an individual. In other words, the figure of the entrepreneur has become not just a type of person but a cultural (and political) ideal. Connell and Wood (2005) are highly critical of that ideal – in part for its dehumanising effects (i.e. transforming the worker into a commodity with a specific – and calculable – monetary value) but also on account of the fact that, like the concept of the 'manager', the entrepreneur turns out to be resolutely gendered (Wee and Brooks, 2012). He (sic) is almost always imagined as someone who is independent, ambitious and willing to take risks.

GENDERING INSTITUTIONS

Thus far in this chapter we have seen that work is gendered in two distinct ways: first, that different jobs are routinely associated with either men or women and, second, that the institutional context of work can also be gendered – in such a way that usually sees men privileged in terms of the ideological 'fit' between masculinity and the image of the worker. However, there is also a third way in which work and gender can be seen to interrelate. The source of these arguments can be traced back to the writings of Karl Marx – which is ironic, given that Marx has been subject to vehement criticism for ignoring gender in his celebrated analyses of capitalist economies. Critics such as Hartmann (1979), Delphy (1984) and Hearn (1987) have all drawn attention to the fact that for Marx, the worker was steadfastly male. The traditional role of women – as wives and housekeepers – had no place in his vision of working-class exploitation and alienation. Nevertheless, at the heart of Marx's writings was a profound contention: that the nature of folk is shaped by the contexts in which they operate. More specifically, Marx claimed that the very character of the worker is a function of their location within the socio-economic system. It is difficult to exaggerate the extent to which such arguments fly in the face of common sense. Most modern companies see recruitment as all about trying to find the right person for the job – and yet, in effect, Marx saw the picture in reverse. For him, working in a factory or mine doesn't just *require* a person with the qualities of strength, tenacity and endurance – it *produces* that sort of character. In more academic parlance, he saw identities as emerging out of the sum of people's everyday 'material' *practices*.

Whilst Marx can in no way be considered an early gender theorist, his *materialist* philosophy is certainly relevant to the field of gender studies. Moss Kanter's book *Men and Women of the Corporation* (Kanter, 1977) is sometimes claimed as the first to explore the implications of Marx's ideas (Leidner, 1991), although a strong case could also be made for Tolson's volume *The Limits of Masculinity* (Tolson, 1977).

Irrespective, the materialist logic underlying these analyses is the same: gender is seen as an artefact of men's and women's respective positioning within the capitalist system. As Marx sought to emphasise, capitalism entails a structure of intensely competitive social relationships. Businesses compete with one another for the greater share of the market; workers compete with each other to get jobs in those businesses – and, via promotions, to rise up through the ranks. But most pointedly of all (for Marx), there is the inevitable competition between employee and employer around wage levels and working conditions. In these ways, capitalism *demands* competitiveness. It renders people as aggressive, defensive, strategic – as well as creative and aspirational. In short, it renders folk as *masculine*. Now, of course, women are also living within the same economic system. However, to the extent that they are engaged in a different set of practices, then, according to this logic, their character and comportment will be at odds with what we find in men. From a materialist point of view, if a woman spends much of her time at home, cooking, cleaning and looking after children, then a different, more 'feminine', type of person will transpire: someone who is caring, compassionate, sensitive and gentle. By the same token, one would expect this to change as women move out of the domestic sphere and enter into the cut and thrust of public life. And indeed many would claim that women *have* changed over the last 60 years, that they have become more assertive and independent – even more aggressive. Yet such transformations tend to be slow. There is a certain inertia around gender, in that it functions to sustain or propagate itself. To illustrate: imagine you phone up a customer-service hotline to complain about a faulty product. It's highly likely that you'll be greeted on the other end of the line by a woman. In many companies and corporations it is assumed that women are best suited to these kinds of job – because it's imagined that, *as* women, they're more likely to have good listening skills, high levels of empathy and, perhaps, a more conciliatory tone. In a way, those companies are probably quite correct: their female employees may indeed possess those sought-after 'soft skills'. But, at the same time, they are also wrong – for it is not *as* women that they possess those particular qualities. From a materialist point of view, that presumption puts the cart before the horse. It would insist that it's not women *per se* who deliver those desired practices; rather, it is the practices themselves that serve to deliver the woman! From a commercial point of view, of course, this difference hardly matters. All companies want is for their customers to put the phone down feeling satisfied (or, at least, brand loyal) – and so they keep on employing women in these roles. Little would they suspect that, in so doing, they may be not just trading on gender differences but actively helping to perpetuate them. Materialist arguments tend to pour cold water on the idea of there being gendered styles of management within organisations. In effect, what they claim is that modern institutions *afford* a particular way of acting as a manager – that the structure and culture of those working environments makes a certain form of conduct the obvious 'way to go' (Wajcman, 1998, dedicates a chapter to this issue, entitled 'It's Hard to be Soft'!). The only reason why it appears as though there might be a masculine style of management is that the vast majority of senior managers are male. Kanter (1977) herself noted that those women who do make it into more senior positions often manage in much the same way. It is not a matter of them trying to be 'one of the boys'; it's just a case of them 'going with the flow' of the organisation once they are in post.

The limited number of women who succeed in breaking through the so-called 'glass ceiling' makes it hard to assess the veracity of those materialist claims, but the forces of globalisation have provided us with another testing ground. Earlier in this chapter, we noted how, over the course of the last four decades, there has been a wholesale collapse in the number of people employed in the old 'heavy' industries; but over that same time period, there has also been a dramatic rise in the number working within the service sector. For example, in England and Wales, this sector alone accounts for the employment of around 80 per cent of all working adults (Office for National Statistics, 2011). Most of those workers will be women; however, millions of them will be men. Writing in the early 1990s, Leidner (1991) explored some of the tensions that exist between masculinity and the ethos of the service industries. She pointed out that in many jobs that involve dealing with customers, what is being sold is as much the salesperson as the product. Workers need to make a good impression on customers; they need to appear friendly, enthusiastic and interested – even if the reality is otherwise. Moreover, as Leidner explained, companies often go to considerable lengths to prepare and control the performances of their customer-facing staff, by issuing uniforms, conducting role-play training exercises and insisting on the use of standardised scripts. In various ways, these demands seem to 'stick in the craw' of many men. As was noted in the previous chapter, the whole idea of putting on a performance for the benefit or amusement of others can sit uneasily with men. However, Leidner suggests that the eagerness to please and fawning insincerity required of these jobs makes them especially uncomfortable for working-class men, whose demeanour tends towards the more down-to-earth and dour. She claims that in the eyes of such men, service work can seem demeaning and effete – and yet, as the figures confirm, many men end up doing these jobs (largely out of necessity). Leidner sought to examine how they coped in these roles. Part of her fieldwork took place in a branch of McDonalds. One of the things that became immediately apparent was the gender division between those working on the grills and those serving on the counters. Although the split was far from absolute, most of the grill workers were male, whereas the majority of the 'window workers' were female. When she enquired about this division she was told, amongst other things, that women were better suited to window work because they were less likely to lose their cool with abusive or difficult customers. It was seen as safer for all concerned if the male employees were deployed elsewhere, other than on the service counters. A second arm of Leidner's research focused on the work of selling insurance door to door. Here, too, employees were tightly schooled in their interactions with customers. Not only were they sent out on to the streets with predetermined scripts, but they were told what to wear, how to stand and even when to deliver the 'standard joke'. Again, the lack of autonomy and the obsequious nature of the role jarred with those same cultural understandings around what it means to be a man. But, unlike at McDonalds, here there was no place to hide. What Leidner discovered was that the salesmen found ways of reimagining their role such that it appeared more in line with those conventions. Their interactions with potential customers (or 'prospects') were construed as a vigorous battle of wills. Accepting the inevitable knock-backs, without outburst or complaint, was framed as a measure of their dogged determination. Amongst the sales team there was a consensus that women lacked the necessary qualities to make it as a successful agent. As one employee commented, 'they don't have the killer instinct'.

From this we can see that Leidner's (1991) research didn't support the idea that men who are drawn into the service sector adopt more feminine forms of working practice. Instead, what it revealed were just some of the strategies that men used to sustain an 'appropriate' gender identity. Indeed, in Leidner's own conclusions, she remarked on the inventiveness shown by people in finding ways to emphasise the congruity between their gender and their work. It seemed to her that almost irrespective of the nature of one's employment, it is possible to give it a masculine (or feminine) gloss. Some support for this thesis can be found in the work of Ramirez (2011), who studied a group of Mexican immigrants tending gardens in the suburbs of Los Angeles. He noted how they were able to put a positive 'spin' on the most demeaning of jobs (for example, picking up dog excrement) by constructing them as being the kind of thing that very few others – male or otherwise – would be willing or able to do. Now, in defence of the materialist stance, it could be said that, irrespective of their nature, the fact that these jobs are embedded within a capitalist culture, where people have to struggle to both get and hold on to any kind of employment, means that the character of the worker will tend towards a more masculine position. However, the same cannot be said for the final area of work to come under our critical spotlight: men's contribution to housework.

As I noted at the beginning of this chapter, housework has often been seen as the epitome of women's work. In my own parents' case, the division was almost absolute. My father died having never put on a clothes wash; the only time he ever used the vacuum cleaner was when he was cleaning out his car; and on those very rare occasions when my mother was away, he'd feed himself by going out to restaurants. However, there are signs that, over the last few decades, the picture is gradually changing. Kan *et al.* (2011) undertook a large-scale review of men's involvement in domestic labour across no less than sixteen developed countries (including Canada, Australia, Israel and the Netherlands). What they discovered was that, over the course of the last 50 years, men appear to have increased their contribution. They reported that, on average, men spend somewhere between two and three hours per day doing domestic chores.

Nevertheless, the authors were careful to stress that women's contribution is still considerably higher (indeed, roughly twice as much), and they also confirmed that the division of labour *within* the domestic sphere appears significantly gendered. They found that women tend to do most of the routine chores, such as the washing, cleaning and ironing, whereas men spend their time on more irregular kinds of activity, like gardening, shopping and DIY. The authors claimed that, in many parts of the world, the kitchen is still seen as very much the woman's domain, which is interesting given that, elsewhere, it has been suggested that twenty-first-century men have a new-found enthusiasm for cooking and food preparation (Miller, 2012; Smith, 2008). In the conclusion of their article, Kan *et al.* (2011) argue that, whilst there are some variations between different countries, the gender gap in domestic work does appear to be narrowing. However, they suggest that this trend has as much, if not more, to do with a general *reduction* in the amount of time women spend working around the home as it does with men's increased preparedness to contribute. One of the major obstacles to change, they argue, is the continued symbolic coding of housework as women's work. Once again, we see evidence of the self-perpetuating nature of masculinity – as men strive to steer clear of any practices incommensurate with society's sense of what it means to be a man.

Yet elsewhere within the same literature, there are voices which sound a more positive or optimistic note with respect to the prospects of significant change. For example, Holter (2007) argues that, within a European context at least, there are signs that the male-as-breadwinner ideal is on the wane. On the basis of 200 interviews with men from countries as diverse as Bulgaria, Austria and Norway, he found that relatively few saw the traditionally gendered division of labour as desirable. Those men who worked long hours (i.e. more than 45 hours per week) tended to resent the fact, rather than seeing it as a good investment of their time; whereas those who worked reduced hours (either part-time or on temporary contracts) tended to view it as an opportunity to achieve a better, more healthy, work/life balance. Like Kan *et al.* (2011), Holter found some regional variations in these patterns: for instance, he found a greater adherence to traditional attitudes in the Mediterranean parts of Europe and a more pro-egalitarian stance within the Scandinavian contingent. And, again like Kan *et al.*, he set about trying to tease apart the main drivers of these trends. He noted, for example, that in the northern, more affluent parts of Europe, there was a greater concentration of service-sector jobs, as opposed to production-based occupations in which more traditional masculinities tend to be anchored. He also explained how the Nordic states have gone further than most in creating legislation that promotes the rights of fathers, as well as mothers, to take time off work to look after their children. Indeed, the laws there seem to recognise that it is not enough just to offer fathers the chance of taking paternity leave. Experience has shown that many men will not avail themselves of the opportunity, even when it is put in front of them, either because they see work as more important or because they fear the consequences, in terms of their careers, if they were to exercise those parental rights. Therefore, in places like Norway and Sweden, they have moved towards making paternal leave more or less compulsory, i.e. 'use it or lose it' (Johansson, 2011). According to the results of Holter's research at least, it seems that men will often come to appreciate the benefits of a more mixed economy of work, once the transition has been made.

Like others working in this field of research, Holter (2007) poses the question of whether these developments are the result of a new generation of men or a new set of circumstances (see also Ranson, 2012). Holter's answer is that it must be a mixture of both. His point about the Swedish paternity laws show how the state can influence the way that men (and women) think about their working lives; but, at the same time, it is clear that people can resist such initiatives. Some of Holter's interviewees spoke of how difficult it had been, in practice, to get their employers to comply fully with state legislation. Others commented on the teasing and taunts that they had been subjected to at the hands of some of their colleagues when they left work 'early' (sic) to spend time with their families. People's attitudes around gender can lag behind and clash with international law and company policies, but there can be little doubt that those institutional forces can also work to change the minds of men. Moreover, it is not just a case of men changing the way that they think about work. It is no coincidence that Holter was engaged on a large EU project entitled 'Work Changes Gender' – for, as we have seen in this chapter, work can be both gendered and gendering. That is, work can be seen as representing both a mechanism for the reproduction of men and masculinity and one of the primary vehicles for their future transformation.

FURTHER READING

Acker, J. (1990) 'Hierarchies, Jobs, Bodies: A theory of gendered organization'. *Gender and Society*, 4: 139–58.
This is one of the defining references for the argument that institutions, as well as people, can be gendered – an important article.

Collinson, D.L. and Hearn, J. (eds) (1996) *Men as Managers, Managers as Men: Critical Perspectives on Men, Masculinities and Management.* London: Sage.
Following on from the work of Acker, this book is a collection of chapters looking at the gendering of work, including emphases on the nature of bureaucracy, entrepreneurialism and the figure of the accountant.

Messerschmidt, J.W. (2003) 'Managing to Kill: Masculinities and the space shuttle Challenger explosion'. In M. Hussey (ed.) *Masculinities: Interdisciplinary Readings.* Upper Saddle River, NJ: Pearson (217–26).
This is a really interesting article, which looks at the US shuttle disaster in terms of a clash of two dominant masculinities.

Tolson, A. (1977) *The Limits of Masculinity.* London: Tavistock.
This is a remarkable book, which appeared a full decade before the broader turn to masculinity at the end of the 1980s. It offers a wonderful insight into the meaning of work for working-class men, in a pre-globalised era.

Connell, R.W. and Wood, J. (2005) 'Globalization and Business Masculinities'. *Men and Masculinities*, 7(4): 347–64.
In this article, the authors look at the emergence of what they call 'transnational business masculinities', i.e. the kind of identities that arise and 'work' within the culture of global corporate enterprises.

5

MEN AND FATHERHOOD

The fact that the last chapter closed around a discussion of men's take-up of paternity leave shows that the themes of work and fatherhood are firmly intertwined. Indeed, the overlap is substantial – and on a number of different levels. As we shall see as this chapter unfolds, the relationship between work and fatherhood is complicated. On the one hand, work has often been viewed as a central component of being a good father; the image of a man as the main provider or breadwinner is still highly relevant across many regions of the world. Yet, in other regards, the same two facets of life are often thought of – and *experienced* – as being in direct *competition* with one another, each making very significant demands on men's time, energy and resources. On a symbolic level, however, work and fatherhood are quite closely aligned. Again, as we heard in the last chapter, the transition from school to work has often been seen as a rite of passage – the moment when the boy becomes a man. Likewise, the transition into fatherhood can mark the same change in status. At the point at which I first became a father, I remember being struck by the number of people who, upon hearing the news, not only offered me their congratulations but who also wanted to shake me by the hand. It was treated as an auspicious event – and I felt as if, in some way, I was being welcomed into the fold.

As I mentioned at the beginning of this book, the issue of fatherhood is one of the more newsworthy topics concerning men and masculinity. The ways that men conduct themselves in relation to their own children is seen as both a cause and symptom of the much talked-about crisis in masculinity. However, the briefest of forays into the wider literature on men and masculinity soon reveals that these grumbles and misgivings are a long-standing feature of Western culture. For instance, Philipson (1981) references an 1842 edition of *Parents Magazine* in which men are berated for spending too much time at work and not enough at home with their children (reported in Lupton and Barclay, 1997). Debates about the role of the father have a long history and, along the way, they have gone through many twists and turns. For instance, it is well documented that in centuries gone by, it was the father who was assumed to be the primary agent in the raising of a child (Pleck, 1987; Gillis, 1995; Stearns, 1991). The role of the mother, by contrast, was reduced to little more than a human incubator. In effect, her contribution was seen as 'done and dusted' once the child was born; thereafter, it was thought to be the father's job to socialise the infant – to discipline, educate and instil a sense of morality. The major shift in this way of thinking was triggered by the onset of industrialisation and the physical separation of work from home (as described in the previous chapter). With the creation of the public and private spheres, many men found themselves spending a significant part of each working day away from the rest of their family. Ideologies (and, in some cases, laws) emerged to justify men's domination of the world of work (Hall, 1992) and, at the same time, there arose another set of arguments which held women to be better suited to meeting the challenges of looking after the kids. Those arguments reached their zenith around the midpoint of the twentieth century, whereupon it was widely imagined that a child's psychological development and well-being required the near constant presence of the mother (Bowlby, 1951). However, since the 1970s, there has been a significant retreat from that quite radical point of view (Rutter, 1972). It is by no means unusual these days to hear people say that women have a more natural affinity for the practices of childcare, but the idea of the father as totally redundant – as the mere provider of seed – has definitely gone out of fashion. Today, there is a growing consensus that fathers ought to be actively involved in their own children's upbringing – and not just as breadwinners. It is widely assumed that fathers need to be more 'hands on' with respect to their kids, for the benefit of all concerned (Lamb, 2004; La Rossa, 1997).

Once again, this turnaround in common-sense thinking can be linked to significant changes in the nature of the global economy (the separation of the two spheres in no way means that public matters don't impinge on private affairs – or vice versa). Compared to the mid twentieth century, one of the key differences in family life is the number of women who now go out to work. Of course, it was never the case that the world of work was a male-only domain. In many working-class families the womenfolk would have had to bring in some kind of income, just to 'make ends meet'. What is different about today's circumstances is not just that the working woman has become a respectable identity within middle-class circles, but also that a significant proportion of middle-class families now require dual incomes to cover the cost of living. Gone are the days when women's wages were seen as 'pin' money, used for treats such as family outings and holidays. The money that they earn is now crucial to the financial security of many households (Dermott, 2008). Of course, it has to be acknowledged that second wave feminism also played a key role in paving the way for these developments. Not surprisingly, feminists were at the forefront of questioning those claims that children needed an omnipresent mother. In their eyes, there was something rather expedient about a theory which, following the cessation of the Second World War, encouraged mothers to abandon paid employment and return to the home. Feminists campaigned long and hard for women to have equal access to the jobs market – and with no little success. In many parts of the developed world, women now work outside of the home for almost as many hours as men (Dermott, 2008).

Over the course of the last four decades, the typical or average family has been transformed in other ways, too. In many of the world's more developed countries, one very clear trend has been a reduction in the overall birth rate. One of the contributing factors is couples leaving it later in life before they embark on having children, but there is also a growing tendency for couples to opt out altogether (to become what some market analysts call 'dinkies', i.e. dual income, no kids). In the Western world at least, the institution of marriage has also come under sustained pressure. Throughout the second half of the twentieth century, there was a sharp increase in the number of couples eschewing marriage – such that in the UK and the US, over 40 per cent of children are now born out of wedlock (in the US, the figure for children born to black women is as high as 70 per cent – see Astone and Peters, 2014). Moreover, for those couples that do marry, the chances of staying together are now considerably lower than they were forty years ago. Again, taking the UK and the US as our prime examples, the current divorce rates stand at somewhere between 40 per cent and 50 per cent. It is well known that a high proportion of those who divorce go on to remarry, but it is also a fact that the rate of attrition for these subsequent unions is higher still.

It hardly needs to be said that these developments carry very serious implications for the relations between children and parents. The vision of the traditional nuclear family, where children spend all of their early years growing up in the company of their biological parents, might remain a staple component of films, books and television sitcoms (Chambers, 2001; Tincknell, 2005), but it describes a diminishing minority of actual living, breathing families (O'Brien, 2004). What the research clearly demonstrates is that, irrespective of the particular family circumstances, the overwhelming majority of children reside with their biological mothers (Astone and Peters, 2014). It is the relationship that children have with their fathers that has been most radically reconfigured over the last forty years. In many parts of the developed world, there has been a steady rise in the number of single-parent households. In the UK (which has a higher rate than most – see Office for National Statistics, 2012), 90 per cent of those lone parents are mothers. Of course, some men father children with no desire or intention of being involved in their lives; however, this is very far from typical. Rather, the fact that so many men live apart from their biological offspring is a consequence of the relatively volatility of contemporary romantic relationships coupled with the social prioritisation of the mother/child bond. There is plenty of evidence to suggest that most men are just as committed to their children as are mothers. For instance, Dermott (2008) reports that, within the UK, 98 per cent of births saw the father in attendance. Likewise, Kiernan et al. (2011) note that, in the UK and the US,

85 per cent of babies born to unmarried parents have the father's name on their birth certificate. Needless to say, in and of themselves, neither of these things guarantees a lifelong commitment to a child, but they do seem to signify some kind of positive intent.

The impermanence of modern coupledom means that many people find themselves in the position of getting into a relationship with somebody who already has a family of their own. Indeed, according to The Step Family Foundation website (www. stepfamily.org), more than half of all American families are now *blended*: that is, made up from fragments of previous relationships. Whilst these families come in all shapes and sizes, there is a predominant pattern – due to the norms of child custody, post-separation. That is, most blended families include a step*father*. Some men's first experiences of parenting are found in such circumstances, but for many others, the role of stepfather comes in *addition* to their prior (and often ongoing) experiences of looking after their own biological offspring. Such complications have led some theorists to distinguish between biological and *social* fathering (Jayakody and Kahil, 2002; Bzostek, 2008), where the latter concept pertains to the actual day-to-day care and support of children. It is all very well, of course, trying to underline the point that fathering means more than just siring a child, but in other respects it is a rather awkward distinction. First, within its own terms, most biological fathers are also social fathers – either to the same or to different sets of children. Second, it begs questions about how one might categorise the traditional father-as-breadwinner. 'Support' comes in many forms, not least in terms of financial provision (indeed, this is often the sole concern of the child support agencies found in places like the US, the UK and Australia). It isn't necessarily hands-on care. If a man works abroad and sends most of his wages home to his wife and family, are we to discount him as a *social* father? As we shall see later on in this chapter, there is a great deal of latitude in terms of what it means to 'be there' for one's kids.

FATHERING AND FATHERHOOD

As part of a study looking into the significance of paid work for British fathers, Shirani *et al.* (2012) make a distinction between *fathering* and *fatherhood*. *Fathering* is defined as the set of everyday practices performed by men in relation to their children – including things like bathing them, picking them up from school and putting them to bed. *Fatherhood*, on the other hand, is offered as something more conceptual. It is defined as a society's collective understanding of what it means to be a father. We can see from this that, whilst distinct, fathering and fatherhood are closely intertwined, in that, for any given period, those shared understandings about the nature of fatherhood will have a direct bearing upon how individual men relate to their children. In a sense, they provide men with a blueprint for their own parental conduct. However, men are not slavish in their response to such prescriptions. As well as falling into line, there is always scope for them to improvise or even to reject those conceptions outright. Moreover, it is sometimes through such acts of innovation and dissent that the prevailing culture shifts. In effect, every successive generation enters into a dialogue with its own culture and, in so doing, moves the 'conversation' along.

It is within this general context that we can start to think a bit more about the fate of the father-as-breadwinner. In doing so it is worth returning to the work of Holter (2007) and his survey of men from across different parts of Europe. As we heard in the last chapter, Holter claimed that there were clear signs of a shift away from equating men with providers. Indeed, he reported that a mere 10 per cent of those surveyed endorsed that particular point of view. It would seem that part of this response was due to the fact that many of Holter's participants saw the situation of dual incomes as 'standard issue'; in other words, they viewed the responsibilities for the family's finances as no longer loaded exclusively on the shoulders of the man. However, there were also signs that work may have changed in terms of its significance for these men. No longer was it seen as their *raison d'être*. Instead, there was evidence of a more *instrumental* attitude towards work. Many spoke of their families as their main priority. Work was viewed as just a means to that end. Interestingly, one commonly heard refrain within the masculinities literature is the suggestion that modern men do not wish to replicate their own father's work/family balance (Lupton and Barclay, 1997; Daly, 1993; Edley and Wetherell, 1999). As far back as the late 1970s, the American writer and psychotherapist Phyllis Chesler (1978) commented on this as a recurrent theme. She noted how young men in particular seemed contemptuous of their own fathers. She wrote:

> More and more, as I listened, it seemed that many men had the same father. *All* the fathers began to merge into one man, one father archetype: a shadow stranger, part tyrant, part failed tyrant . . . an awkward man, uneasy or out of place at home.
>
> (Chesler, 1978: 200; original emphasis)

Of course, if we do the maths, we can see that many of Chesler's clients would have been describing their experiences of family life in 1950s America, at a time when the notion of the separate spheres for men and women (i.e. public and private) was at its height. The fact that today's fathers are calling for a different kind of settlement reflects a marked shift in the concept of fatherhood, brought about not just by transformations in the nature of the global economy but also as a reaction to the impact of those previous superstructural arrangements on the day-to-day lives of ordinary families.

Whatever forces lie behind the transition from father-as-breadwinner to the new (or renewed), more involved, or hands-on, father, there is no doubt that many men today both expect and are expected to engage with their children to an extent that would never have applied to their own fathers or grandfathers. Moreover, there is evidence to back up the suggestion that fathering practices have indeed changed over the course of the last few decades. In fact, Bittman (2004) claimed that the average time that American fathers spent with their children had doubled since the mid 1970s. One has to be careful around such statistics, however, because they tend to gloss over what is a highly complex picture. For instance, as we have already heard, during that same timeframe, there has been a sharp rise in the prevalence of single mothers; and whilst that doesn't necessarily translate into an equivalent number of *feckless* fathers (not least because, in some studies, 'single' simply means unmarried), it is the case that there are more men today who are dislocated from the lives of their own children. In other words, the last forty years have witnessed *polarised* trends around fatherhood, rather than a wholesale shift towards greater involvement (Dermott, 2008; Taylor and Behnke, 2005). Other research has shown that levels of fatherly involvement vary according to geographical region (Lamb, 2004; Holter, 2007; Seward and Richter, 2008) and also by social class (Warren, 2003; Craig, 2006), but again in complex ways. Several critics have pointed to the discrepancies between the ideals of fatherhood and the realities of what men actually do (Machin, 2015; Dermott, 2008), but how men father is not just a reflection of their own volition or commitment. Rather, it is something that emerges out of a subtle negotiation amongst a whole range of different factors.

There is no doubt that one of the most important considerations is the balance struck between family life and paid employment. As we have heard, more and more families today rely on two incomes rather than just that of the father. Moreover, it is still the case that, whilst women have made significant strides in gaining a foothold in the jobs market, men still work more hours per week than women and, on average, earn more for the hours they spend at work (Connell, 2009; World Economic Forum, 2015). Therefore, when it comes to the point of couples trying to decide who, if at all, is going to take time out of their careers to look after the children, more often than not it falls to the woman, on what would appear to be purely economic grounds. Of course, such decisions don't always see women giving up entirely on paid employment. Rather, a common pattern sees them going part-time. Furthermore, it seems that organisations are often more open to women making this transition insofar as it fits in with preconceptions about the priority of the mother/child relationship (Wajcman, 1998).

For many years, those selfsame preconceptions have been institutionalised in terms of both state legislation and company policies around parental leave. As O'Brien (2004) points out, prior to the early 1970s, most European countries made no provision at all for fathers to take time off work after the birth of a child. By the end of the millennium, numerous member states offered men some statutory leave – usually a matter of just a few days – whereas mothers were often entitled to several months away from the workplace. One could argue, of course, that mothers need more time off work given the rigours of the birthing process, but the fact is that the respective timeframes not only gave a very clear steer as to who was assumed to be acting as the primary carer, but they also made it practically difficult for couples to confound those presumptions. By contrast, the Nordic countries of Sweden, Norway and Demark have a much more established tradition of gender equality in terms of their arrangements for parental leave. As I outlined in the last chapter, not only do they offer parents the opportunity to share a block of time away from work, but they also give fathers a dedicated period of leave (the so-called 'daddy month') which is not transferable to the mother (Johansson, 2011). Historically, in most countries around the developed world, the take-up of paternal leave has been conspicuously low. For example, O'Brien (2004) reported that, outside of the Nordic bloc, the figure was usually below 5 per cent. Amongst the most common justifications for not taking up the allowance was the loss of the father's income, a hostile or unsympathetic employer and a sense that the mother was better suited to looking after the child in any case! Amongst all of these considerations, one must not lose sight of another crucial factor in this highly complex equation: the wishes and desires of *mothers*. A great deal has been written about men's reluctance (and indeed resistance) in meeting women halfway in terms of domestic work and childcare, but there is also evidence that many mothers do not want or welcome a reduction in the amount of time spent looking after their children (Lamb and Tamis-LeMonda, 2004). Few, no doubt, would be found barring the door to the utility room or concealing the dishcloths and polish, but, like an increasing number of fathers, mothers see time with their children as both precious and a priority.

BECOMING A FATHER

Later on in this chapter, I want to examine the issue of what impact fathers have on the lives of their children. In particular, I want to address the question of whether fathers offer something unique, something that cannot be supplied by a mother. But first, in this section, I want to look at the impact of becoming a father on men themselves. One might imagine that, back in the mid twentieth century, the consequences of becoming a father were somewhat different compared to today. To the extent that Chesler's (1978) portrait is accurate, it would seem that many men's engagement was both short in duration and superficial in character. Indeed, insofar as fatherhood was then dominated by the image of the breadwinner, becoming a father would often see men spending even less time at home, as they redoubled their efforts to consolidate their earning potential. This isn't to suggest, of course, that fathers back then were entirely indifferent to the welfare of their children; rather, it is to say that they way that they interpreted and experienced that new role was largely through the prism and practices of work.

As we have seen, in today's context, men are expressing a much greater interest in 'being there' for their children. But what this actually means is open to interpretation. For example, Forste *et al.* (2009) found that, for some men, it translates into being just a reliable provider: someone who works hard, and possibly long hours, to support their family. For others, it marks a clear shift *away* from an emphasis on work and towards a determination to be more present and involved in the day-to-day rhythms of family life. In response to this desire for greater intimacy, gender researchers have set out to examine men's feelings around their lives as fathers. One of the most striking features of their findings is the emotional intensity with which men speak about their experiences. The established literature on men and masculinity is replete with claims that men are emotionally stunted, that they are alienated from their own feelings and largely incapable of putting their feelings into words (Brittan, 1989; Clare, 2000; Horrocks, 1994; Rutherford, 1988; Whitehead, 2002). Such arguments sit awkwardly with the data from these more recent studies. Gattrell (2007), for example, quotes one father who said that witnessing the birth of his child was 'just the most wonderful experience ever'. Another (quoted in Dermott, 2008) described it as 'magical' and went on: '[the baby] wasn't like a human being she was like a gift from god or something, like an angel'. Solomon (2014) reports that several of her interviewees began to cry as they spoke about the joys of looking after their children, and both Dermott (2008) and Lupton and Barclay (1997) make reference to fathers describing their relations with their children as like falling 'head over heel in love'.

It is little wonder, therefore, that the transition to fatherhood has been seen as a transformative event (Roy, 2006), propelling men away from the routines of a more self-centred life and into an entirely different orbit. Here are the words of another father, as reported by Forste *et al.* (2009):

> When you have a child, that child is depending on you. [ ] You have to put the child first. [ ] There's a bit of selflessness in being a parent.

> If you have a child and your think you're going to have your cake and eat it too, then you'll be a bad parent.
>
> (61–2)

Ashbourne *et al.* (2011) claim that the transition to fatherhood provides men with what they call a strong 'future orientation'. That is to say, it brings about a profound shift in the temporal framework through which men view their own lives. When a baby is born, the child invokes the future. The minds of the parents are cast forward in anticipation of the various milestones that lie ahead: her first steps, his first words, their first day at school. Moreover, the parents' own lives are similarly recalibrated. That sense of wanting to 'be there' for the child sees them projected forward in time. They envisage themselves collecting the child from school, taking them camping, teaching them to swim and so on and so forth. Their outlook is extended away from a focus on just the here and now. But, as it turns out, it is more than just men's *outlook* that is transformed by becoming a father. There is evidence from numerous studies which suggests that it can extend their very lives! As Astone and Peters (2014) explain, the reasons behind this effect could be many and varied. Some have suggested that, as fathers, men tend to engage in less risky forms of behaviour (Eggebeen *et al.*, 2013). Another hypothesis is that with children comes an extended network of social contacts – as well as an intensification of existing family ties (i.e. as siblings become aunts and uncles and parents turn into grandparents), which both serve to bolster the support that fathers (and, of course, mothers too) receive. However, Astone and Peters (2014) note that these positive effects on men's health and well-being are largely restricted to those who live with their children. The benefits for those men who father remotely are much less obvious. It may well be that it is not children *per se* that extend a father's life but the therapeutic effects of a stable family environment.

Yet, in spite of these research findings, it is still the case that, in most parts of the world, children spend more time with their mothers than they do with their fathers. In a survey of 14 European countries, Smith (2004) concluded that, of the standard childcare duties, men's contribution was nowhere above 30 per cent of the workload. The signs are that the gap is closing, but, as with the trends around housework in general, this has more to do with a reduction in the number of hours that mothers now spend with their children than with a significant rise in the level of men's involvement (Lamb, 2004). So how can we reconcile this wave of enthusiasm about the prospect of fathering with the rather modest changes in the way that men are engaging with their children? Is it all just bluff and bluster or is there something else going on? One study which may help shed some light upon this question comes in the form of a paper by Shirani *et al.* (2012). The focus of their study was on a series of interviews with first-time fathers who were in non-standard employment situations: either as unemployed, home-employed or full-time stay-at-home dads. All of these men spent a significant amount of time with their young children and could be easily thought of as modern, 'involved' fathers. But in one way or another, each of them was made to feel the normative pressures of the more traditional ideal (i.e. the father-as-breadwinner). Some of the men described the quizzical looks they'd receive from strangers when they were out during the day with their children. Others spoke of the incredulity of friends, work colleagues and even members of their own families when they announced that they'd be giving up their jobs and assuming the role of house-husband. But sometimes the pressures come as much from within as from without. Such was the case for a character they identified as 'Eric'. Eric was on a short-term research contract when his daughter was born, but some months later he found himself unemployed. For him, it was an unsettling period. In an earlier interview, Eric had very much endorsed the idea that parental roles were interchangeable. It didn't matter who was the breadwinner, he said, 'It's just family income'. And yet when he found himself in the position of being at home with his daughter, whilst his wife went out to work, he was far from content. His disgruntlement was a surprise to himself. He remarked:

> I always thought I was quite a liberal modern man and suddenly you feel very upset that you can't provide for your family. I really feel strong that both kind of financially but also emotionally I'm there for my family. And that was quite difficult not having a job and not feeling, feeling I was kind of being dependent on them rather than they being dependent on me.

> (Shirani *et al.*, 2012: 278)

In time, Eric resumed paid employment but at some distance from home. The time spent at work and on the road made him anxious about the impact on his relationship with his daughter. During the week, she'd be asleep when he left the house and in bed again when he returned home in the evening. Nevertheless, he said he enjoyed bonding with her at the weekends, during which time his wife committed herself to work. Years later, Eric again changed jobs and, this time, the whole family relocated so that he would be spared the long commute. His wife gave up her job and assumed a more traditional role of mother and housekeeper. It was a settlement that was stable but by no means perfect. Although happy at work, Eric expressed misgivings about not being the kind of father he'd wanted to be. Moreover, he reported that his wife had found the transition tough. He explained:

> Suddenly you're only a mother to Phoebe or the wife to the husband who is working rather than being an economic entity in yourself . . . which came quite hard I must say.
>
> (Shirani *et al.*, 2012: 279)

What shines through these accounts is that Eric (and possibly his wife too) is caught in the grip of an *ideological dilemma* (Billig *et al.*, 1988). He wants to be an 'involved', or hands-on, dad, but at the same time he wants to be the provider (Yarwood, 2011). Such evidence makes us think again about the claim made by Holter (2007) that fathers are turning away from the role of the breadwinner. As we can see here, it is not an 'all or nothing' thing. If there is a sea change under way then it is a gradual process, during which time men can be found identifying with *both* ideals simultaneously. The problem (or dilemma) is, of course, that, on a practical level, it is hard to do both things at once. Most men have to commit to one or the other role – and then, like Eric perhaps, live with a measure of consternation and regret. The current statistics would suggest that, in the face of this predicament, the majority of men in the developed world end up gravitating towards the traditional gender arrangements (Machin, 2015). However, there are signs that a growing number of fathers are adopting the alternative 'solution': that is, opting to become stay-at-home dads. For various reasons it is hard to be sure about the extent of the rise of these 'SAHDs', but the suggestion is that, in countries like the UK and the US, the numbers have doubled over the course of the last twenty-five years (Solomon, 2014).

In the above paper by Solomon (2014), she notes that there have been a number of studies on the phenomenon of SAHDs. In particular, she highlights the work of Andrea Doucet (2006) and Noelle Chesley (2011). In both of these earlier studies, it was found that SAHDs tended to *fall* into the role of house-husband as a result of some kind of 'shock' or interruption to their routine of being a provider. For example, some men had been sacked or made redundant, whereas others had resigned their jobs in order to allow their families to relocate following some change in their wives' career-paths. To that extent, many saw their situation as something of a stopgap, rather than it being a permanent or long-term arrangement. As with Shirani *et al.* (2012), both researchers heard how these men met with a level of social disapproval, treated as if they were suspect or just poor substitutes for a proper mother. Furthermore, both Doucet and Chesley noted that these men would often engage in activities that seemed designed to compensate for the damage done to their sense of masculinity. Not only did some of them take up part-time jobs, but they also seemed to invest themselves disproportionately in the more 'manly' aspects of their roles as SAHDs, such as doing DIY, tending to the garden or participating in sporting activities. By contrast, Solomon (2014) claims that amongst her sample of SAHDs, there was evidence of a much more positive engagement with the role. Most of the men she interviewed spoke of it as being an active choice rather than a situation that came to them by accident. For some, the decision to stay at home had followed the loss of a job, but the difference here was that they saw this as a prompt or opportunity to do something they had long wished for. Moreover, unlike those previous studies, Solomon's interviewees spoke at length about the positive responses they had received from others, including encounters with other men who wished that they could do (or had done) the same.

For the most part, Solomon accepts her respondents' words at face value. As such, she interprets her own findings as a positive sign of things to come, where men have relinquished those rigid prescriptions around the role of the father. And, of course, things have changed. In a world where so many mothers work and where their earnings can sometimes outstrip those commanded by men, family life is bound to be different. And yet, if we look more closely at her interviewees' accounts of their lives as fathers, we can see, once again, clear evidence of their attempts to *rationalise* their own situations – to make them appear to fit in with standard (or hegemonic) under-standings of what it means to be a man (Leidner, 1991). The insist-ence that becoming a SAHD was their *choice* is a case in point, insofar as it positions the man as a free agent and author of his own destiny. The claim by another participant, that his son was 'six books ahead of his entire class' (Solomon, 2014: 64), can be seen as a tale of his own efficacy as a father and, as such, a sign of his competitiveness. Likewise, when a character called 'Theo' described the moment that he took on the role of a SAHD, it is not insignificant (surely) that he framed it as being driven by a desire to 'take care' of his wife and daughter (Solomon, 2014: 58). In his account, the fact that he would be living off her wages seems to recede into the background. In line with the traditional narratives, it is she who is constructed as being dependent upon him, not the other way around.

DO FAMILIES NEED FATHERS?

It is clear from the above that becoming a father has a significant impact upon a man. For some, a son or daughter will be experienced mainly as a burden, an unwanted responsibility and drain upon his financial resources. But, for the much larger majority, having chil-dren is a 'game-changer' or 'signal event' (Holter, 2007). In many parts of the world, it confers status upon the man, and it also brings new meaning, structure and purpose to men's lives. Several authors have noted how men view their children as their *legacy* – a way of leaving a mark upon the world in terms of the transmission of their own values and ideals (Ashbourne *et al.*, 2011; Marsiglio, 2009; Lupton and Barclay, 1997). As we have also heard, becoming a father opens the door to a range and depth of emotional experiences that are seldom found in any other area of a man's life. However, what about the view from the other side of the fence? Presidents and prime ministers may point their fingers at 'feckless' fathers or 'deadbeat' dads as the root cause of so many social ills amongst the young: vandalism, drug-addiction, truancy from school – but what are the facts? Is the campaign group Families Need Fathers correct in its founding assumption? What difference do fathers make to the lives of their offspring and, in particular, do they provide anything distinctive over and above the contributions made by mothers?

Given the political charge surrounding these debates, it should come as no surprise to hear that there has been a tremendous amount of research done in this area. The weighty tome that is Michael Lamb's edited collection *The Role of the Father in Child Development,* first published in 1976, is now in its fifth edition (2010). In the preface to the fourth volume (2004), Lamb notes that the first two editions were dedicated to the task of trying to establish whether or not fathers had a significant impact upon the development of their kids. By the time the third and fourth editions were published, he said, that question had been put to bed; the fact of their influence was now established beyond doubt. Attention turned instead to exploring global variations in fathering practices, the differential experiences of particular subgroups, such as African American dads, gay dads and working-class dads, and social policy and legislative changes around paternal rights and responsibilities. But let's rewind a little: what difference does a father make to the upbringing of a child?

Across this substantial literature, one of the most trenchant appeals for taking seriously the impact of fathers on the development of children comes in the form of Dennis and Erdos's (2000) book, *Families without Fatherhood*. Here the authors claim, in no uncertain terms, that the traditional set-up of the nuclear family is the optimal arrangement for ensuring children's health and well-being. Indeed, they go so far as to suggest that, without this particular family background, children will be more prone to illness, more likely to fail at school, more likely to find themselves in trouble with the law and destined to die at a younger age! Less spectacularly, other researchers have confirmed that fathers do make a difference. Amongst the various claims, it has been said that their involvement sees children enjoying greater self-control, more empathy and a heightened sense of their own agency or efficacy (Pleck, 1997; Pruett, 2000; see also Allen and Daly, 2007). However, one of the problems with much of this research is that it is based upon *correlational* studies. In other words, it draws upon research where the competencies, qualities and abilities of children are measured and compared between those situations where a father is present and those where he is absent. The problem is that, in such cases, it is notoriously difficult to establish *causal* links or relationships. For example, whilst it is certainly plausible that a father's influence might reduce the likelihood of disruptive behaviour in a child, it is just as possible that a troublesome child could be the reason (or at least one of the reasons) why a man packs his bags and leaves. In both scenarios, we are left with 'difficult child' + 'absent father', but we cannot know for sure what causes what.

Although it is by no means always the case, an absent father often means that children are being cared for by a single mother. Therefore, comparisons between children who have fatherly input versus those bereft of it are often recording the differences between having two parents as opposed to just one. As every parent knows, looking after children can be a demanding and time-consuming business, and, compared to a couple, a single mother is always going to find it tougher to find the time and energy to cover all that needs to be done. Moreover, it is very well established that single mothers are amongst the least affluent members in society, often surviving on either state benefits or part-time earnings (or a mixture of both), supplemented, perhaps, by maintenance contributions from the biological father (Amato and Sobolewski, 2004). There is little doubt that some of the effects attributed to growing up without a father are, in fact, the consequences of living in relative poverty. What is more, society affords us an obvious way of testing this hypothesis – by looking at the developmental consequences of children raised by lesbian couples. What research there is suggests that, on all kinds of measures, children fair just as well as when they are brought up by heterosexual parents (Farr *et al.*, 2010; Goldberg, 2009; Tasker and Patterson, 2007).

In the introduction to the piece by Farr *et al.* (2010), the authors note the widespread concerns that have been expressed in the past about the ability of same-sex couples to bring up children with stable gender identities. Groups like *Families Need Fathers* claim that boys, in particular, require the involvement of a father if they are to grow up into mature, fully functioning men. In essence, their argument is that boys need an appropriate figure upon which to model themselves. However, as Lamb and Tamis-LeMonda (2004) report, despite significant efforts, gender researchers have found no clear evidence of a link between the gender identities of fathers and sons. In other words, boys are by no means always a 'chip off the old block'. Indeed, they go on to conclude that 'very little about the gender of the parent seems to be distinctly important' (Lamb and Tamis-LeMonda, 2004: 6). But how do we square such a claim with the earlier assertions that fathers do make a difference? Surely there is a contradiction.

The key to this apparent conundrum begins with the recognition that, in most parts of the world, there is an unequal division of labour between mothers and fathers in terms of childcare duties. As we have already heard, across Europe, men's engagement falls significantly below the levels performed by women (Smith, 2004), and the same can be said of families in the US (Pleck and Masciadrelli, 2004) and in many parts of Asia (Shwalb *et al.*, 2004). But the differences are not just to do with the relative proportions of the work shouldered by the father and the mother; it is also an issue of the specific duties undertaken by each. Numerous studies have shown that, just as with their involvement in domestic chores (Chapter 4), men tend to steer clear of the more mundane aspects of childcare (Dermott, 2008; Machin, 2015). Some would argue that they cherry pick the more palatable or enjoyable activities – such as playing games with the children and reading to them before bedtime. Indeed, such impressions are backed up by the evidence gained from various time-diary studies (Bittman, 2004). The point is that, insofar as mothers and fathers engage their children in different activities, they will make differential contributions to their social and psychological development. For instance, it has often been noted that, compared to mothers, fathers are much more likely to engage their children in 'rough and tumble' play (Carson and Parke, 1996; Lindsey *et al.*, 1997). This is often linked to the idea that, as men, fathers are more aggressive than mothers. However, this kind of play is also seen as promoting certain desirable qualities in children, such as confidence and self-control. Therefore, we can see how easy it is to jump to the conclusion that children *need* fathers in order to derive those kinds of developmental benefit. But the question is: are fathers uniquely equipped to instil these qualities? Or, to put it another way: are mothers constitutionally incapable of engaging in rough-and-tumble play?

A number of these other dads have said that they find what I'm about to say similar. That I'll be home with the kid all day and dad doesn't – myself included – doesn't have the typical father–kid or father–son play with the kid. That we don't wrestle with our kids because we don't have that need, we don't have to squish play into a two-hour period between the end of a workday and bedtime. So you don't have that intense quality play with your kid. And on the flip side, that mom will get home after a long work day and mom in an uncharacteristic way will walk in the door and will want to wrestle on the floor with the kid and have this very tactile intense power play, engaged play which the dad is like, 'Wow, I've never really seen this before. Where is this coming from? Because I wouldn't have expected this'. I have to consciously think, 'I should wrestle with my son'.

('Luke', taken from Solomon, 2014: 62)

Luke was just one of Catherine Solomon's sample of stay-at-home dads, and it would be easy to write off his experiences as eccentric or idiosyncratic. However, there are other sources of evidence which support the suggestion that rough-and-tumble play is not an expression of paternal or manly instincts. Hewlett (1991) conducted a study of the Aka tribe from Central Africa – a group of hunter-gatherers – and he witnessed virtually no sign of rough-and-tumble play between fathers and their children. Similar to Luke, the menfolk of the Aka remain in close physical proximity to their children for most of the day and, as Hewlett notes, develop an intimate under-standing of their ways and needs. What this implies, of course, is that rough-and-tumble play isn't a masculine style of parenting *per se* but a mode of parental engagement which emerges when time with the child is limited. It is a practice sustained not by the minds and bodies of men, but by the gendering of the public and private spheres.

But if we look again at the quotation from Luke, we should see that it raises a second, related, question, albeit one that is posed much less frequently: do families need *mothers*? Such a question sounds peculiar because common sense leads us to imagine, of course, that mothers are *natural* parents – that caring for others is part of their very make-up (NB we speak only of maternal, not paternal, instincts). However, there is strong evidence to support Lamb and Tamis-LeMonda's (2004) contention that the gender of the parent is largely irrelevant in terms of the health and happiness of children. Research looking at gay dads (Farr *et al.*, 2010; Goldberg, 2009), single dads (Risman, 1986) and stay-at-home dads (Solomon, 2014; Grbich, 1995) seems to point to the same conclusion – that, given sufficient time and space, the parenting of men is hard to distinguish from what we think of as 'mothering'.

FURTHER READING

Clare, A. (2000) 'Man the Father'. In *On Men: Masculinity in Crisis*. London: Chatto and Windus (161–93).

In this chapter, the renowned psychiatrist takes a look at some of the changes in recent thinking about fatherhood and considers some of the psychological consequences of parenting for both fathers and their children.

Dermott, E. (2008) *Intimate Fatherhood: A Sociological Analysis*. London: Routledge.

This is an excellent review of the situation of many modern fathers living in the Western world. Dermott looks at various trends and historical patterns in the practices of fathers and pays particular attention to how men meet the dilemma of being both providers and yet still 'there' for their children.

Edley, N. and Wetherell, M. (1999) 'Imagined Futures: Young men's talk about fatherhood and domestic life'. *British Journal of Social Psychology*, 38(2): 181–94.

This analysis puts the spotlight on a keen dilemma for the modern man: how to reconcile work and childcare. It examines the ideological dimensions underpinning this now common conundrum.

Lamb, M.E. (ed.) (2010) *The Role of the Father in Child Development* (5th. edition). Hoboken, NJ: Wiley & Sons.

Now in its fifth edition, this book has become one of the core references in the study of fathers and fatherhood. It is both comprehensive in its coverage and global in its scope.

Solomon, C.R. (2014) '"I Feel Like a Rock Star": Fatherhood for stay-at-home fathers'. *Fathering*, 12(1): 52–70.

This is an interesting study of men who make an active decision to go for 'role reversal' and become primary childcarers. In outlining their experiences, the article also serves to underline those arguments about the interchangeability of mothering and fathering.

6

MALE SEXUALITY

Of all the different facets of men's lives covered in this book, the focus on sexuality provides, I think, the sternest challenge. The problem isn't a lack of resources; indeed, as Attwood (2006) points out, the latter part of the twentieth century witnessed a rapid increase in the number of academics turning their attention to the subject of men's (and women's) sexuality. Rather, the issue is more one of 'disciplinarity' – or the fact that this rapidly expanding literature features a clash of theoretical perspectives which poses trouble for any attempt at synthesis. Without doubt, one of the prime resources for thinking about male sexuality has been psychoanalytic theory (or theories). As we saw in Chapter 2, Freud's writings about human sexuality go back much further than the last few decades. In fact, for most of the twentieth century, psychoanalysis was almost alone in providing a theoretical account of men's desires, fantasies and sexual practices. Moreover, psychoanalytic explanations retain their currency, with some of the most pre-eminent voices in the field of masculinity studies making routine use of arguments derived either directly or indirectly from Freud. For example, in the writings of Connell (1995), Messner (2010) and Seidler (1989) we see it suggested that men's intimate lives are coloured significantly by anxieties stirred up, as boys, within the phallic stage of psychosexual development.

There are a number of reasons why psychoanalytic explanations maintain their contemporary appeal. One is that they seem to capture the vitality of human sexuality. As we've heard, psychoanalysis speaks of irresistible urges and powerful emotions, which, for many commentators, seem to be a palpable component of people's romantic and erotic experiences. Another draw is the notion of the unconscious. Folk are often at a loss to explain why some people make them weak at the knees whilst others leave them cold. Even more mysterious is the bewildering array of sexual predilections that human beings exhibit. Only a few months ago, a programme aired on one of the UK's mainstream television channels which sought to 'lift the lid' on the sex lives of the British public. Amongst other things, *The Great British Sex Survey* (Channel 4) showcased one man who liked to wander around the countryside clad in an extravagant black latex suit and another who had a penchant for immersing his penis in a jar full of worms! Many of these so-called *paraphilia* have their own classificatory designation (see Wikipedia for a list of such terms), including: apotemnophilia (an erotic attraction to amputees), coprophilia (the love of faeces) and oculolinctus (taking sexual pleasure from licking people's eyeballs). When it comes to matters of sexuality and eroticism, there seems to be much that is quite beyond reason.

At the same time, however, there are also reasons to be wary of psychoanalytic explanations. Apart from their fantastical qualities, the theories that derive from the work of Freud offer a universal model of humankind, which sees the nature of folk as being the same across all times and places. For Freud, sexuality lay at the heart of what it was to be a person; he saw it as part of our very essence. Of course, it is quite likely that many readers would agree with Freud on this point. In other words, they would share the conviction that our sexuality is 'the most spontaneously natural thing about us' (Weeks, 1986: 13). However, the position advanced within this chapter comes out of an alternative theoretical stance, one that understands that same conviction, not as the expression of some eternal truth but as a reflection of this particular moment in history. Central to these arguments is the work of Gagnon and Simon (1973) and Michel Foucault (1979). Here isn't the place to go into the details of these pioneering studies. The important point to take from them is the idea that human sexuality is not something that sits outside of society (or indeed *against* it, as Freud suggested), but something that is produced in and through social processes. As various authors have pointed out, there is a great deal of variation between cultures in terms of sexuality (Plummer, 2003). Weeks (1986) claims that in some parts of the world, very little is made of it, whereas in regions such as Europe and the US, we live now in highly sexualised environments. Moreover, as Weeks goes on to explain, sexuality is structured by things like class and ethnicity (i.e. there are systematic differences in the sexual activities of middle- and working-class folk, as well as between blacks and whites – even between members of different national groups). In this sense, sexuality seems far from being a universal expression of underlying biological impulses. Rather, it appears as something intensely social and/or cultural.

THE HISTORY OF SEXUALITY

It goes without saying that human beings have always had sex. What the history of sexuality concerns itself with is the issue of how, over time, sex has been variously understood. What is more, it looks at how those different understandings help to shape the nature of sexual practices, as well as the emotions and desires that wrap around or attend those same activities. For example, in spite of the fact that we live in an era of supposed sexual liberation or enlightenment, there is no doubt that sex continues to carry a sense of something transgressive or taboo. The fact that many of us live in highly sexualised cultures does little to diminish the idea that sex is something risqué, naughty, even dangerous. Indeed, the hyper-visibility of sexuality in contemporary society trades, quite literally, upon these common associations. Of course, for Freud, the transgressive nature of sex is anchored in the psychology of every individual, as a consequence of their early incestuous desires. However, according to various historians of sex, the origins of these taboos go much further back in time. Gagnon and Simon (1973) argue that the roots can be traced back more than 2000 years, to the first century AD. Their claim is that some of the early Christian tribes, concerned with their own viability, created a law forbidding a man from 'spilling his seed' in any way except through heterosexual intercourse. They decreed that to transgress was to sin against God. Over the ensuing centuries, as the influence of Christianity spread across the globe, so did the reach of the so-called *coital imperative* (i.e. the notion that the only 'real', or 'legitimate', form of sex is sexual intercourse). What's more, the power of that imperative still remains remarkably strong today. Indeed, in her monumental survey of male sexuality, the feminist writer Shere Hite would record men saying things like: 'It is sinful to ejaculate anywhere but in my wife's vagina' (Hite, 1990: 419).

The impact of Christian doctrine on the contours of male sexuality has been a major theme in the writing of Victor Seidler (1989, 2000). According to Seidler, as well as helping to propagate the coital imperative, Christianity has had an enduring influence upon contemporary attitudes towards sex. As we heard in Chapter 3, Seidler argues that we in the West inherit from our Judaeo-Christian heritage a sense that sex belongs to the realm of the body; that it is something lowly or profane, far removed from the vaunted domains of the intellect and spirit. Lust, of course, is also listed as one of the seven deadly sins, and, within the Christian church, the institution of marriage has often been seen as a means of containing, or restraining, libidinal energies and desires that, if left unchecked, might threaten our mortal souls. As sex was deemed to be purely for the purpose of procreation, sex for its own sake (i.e. for pleasure) was condemned as the devil's work – the sin of *fornication*. And yet, looking back through the history of (Western) sexuality, one is struck not just by the longevity of certain ideas, but also by the way in which other understandings have shifted over time. For instance, Weeks (1986) points out that up until the eighteenth century, it was widely assumed that the fires of lust burned most brightly within the loins of women. Just as in the book of Genesis, women were viewed as the most likely cause of a man's 'fall from grace'. It was men, in particular, who were seen as in need of spiritual guidance and religious fortitude to steel themselves against the siren calls of the female sex. But then, for much of the nineteenth and twentieth centuries, the thinking ran the other way. Now it was *men* who were thought to have the more active, or predatory, sexuality. Indeed, Weeks claims that in Victorian England, women were portrayed as being almost bereft of sexual desire. These days, of course, we tend to imagine that both sexes are endowed with a similar sexual appetite, or that it is something that varies between individuals rather than across the sexes as a whole.

This long and somewhat turbulent history of sexuality leaves us today in a situation where our own common sense is a mixture of modern ideas shot through with themes that stem from centuries past (as demonstrated by the quote from Hite, 1990, above). As a consequence, Seidler (1989) argues, men have a complicated, even ambiguous, relationship with their own sexuality. They may well be active and enthusiastic in their pursuit of sexual experiences, but at the very same time they can be profoundly threatened or unsettled by what they encounter along the way. As we have already seen (Chapter 3), men have an ambivalent relationship with their own bodies, and it is around sex, perhaps, where these tensions are at their most acute. Seidler claims that men like to feel in *control* of their own bodies, but that in sexual relations that sense of mastery is often hard to sustain. In the UK during the 1980s, cartoonist Gray Jolliffe produced a highly successful series of books about a penis/character called Wicked Willie. The first volume was entitled *Man's Best Friend*, but this was largely a misnomer – for most of the humour in these books revolved around the fact that Willie was not to be trusted. Depending upon how he was feeling, he was just as capable of failing to come to the party as he was showing up uninvited.

Of course, as with most humour, there is a serious side to these funny stories. As mentioned in the opening chapter, millions of men worldwide are currently taking the drug Viagra (or one of its commercial alternatives – for example, Cialis and Levitra) to improve their virility. Not all of these men are suffering from erectile dysfunctions. Indeed, an increasing number of healthy young men (i.e. many in their teens and early twenties) are taking these drugs in the hope of gaining bigger, harder and longer lasting erections. In a very real sense, this billion-dollar industry is the direct cost of men's insecurities about their abilities to perform.

In her writings about men, Phyllis Chesler (1978) also raised the issue of performance anxiety. Having interviewed many men on the details of their intimate lives, she concluded that what they seemed to enjoy most about sex was having it 'over and done with' – especially when they believed that they had acquitted themselves well. She reported that most of her interviewees expressed a preference for 'quickies', i.e. coital intercourse with little or no foreplay, and that, afterwards, many experienced what the French call *la petit mort*: that is, a feeling of post-coital disappointment, loneliness and even a vague sense of disgust. Seidler (1989), no doubt, would see these reactions as evidence of the continued impact of those same age-old traditions which hold sex in such low esteem – where the desire for sex is experienced as weakness and the act itself degrading. Likewise, he would see men's penchant for quickies as an attempt to minimize the degree of intimacy involved with sex, because, he maintains, emotions are also antithetical to Western notions of hegemonic masculinity. Seidler claims that intimacy threatens men's gender identities, as it lands them in the midst of the irrational. In experiencing feelings such as jealousy, longing and lust, men often feel compromised: vulnerable, dependent and hopelessly out of control.

But there are other writers who would argue that men's anxieties around sex are of much more recent origin. For example, David Cohen (1990) claims that the women's liberation movement of the 1960s and 70s played a significant role in raising those concerns. At that time, he said, feminists had begun speaking quite openly about the realities of heterosexual sex. Shere Hite's earlier survey of *female* sexuality (Hite, 1976) played a crucial role in making public American women's feelings and experiences. She broke the news that the majority of women (around 70 per cent) didn't usually achieve orgasm through conventional intercourse – even though most were able to do so via other forms of stimulation (her survey also exposed hitherto unsuspected levels of erectile dysfunction in men). In the face of such evidence, second wave feminists began to call for women to strive for sexual satisfaction, either in relationships or independently (Duncombe and Marsden, 1996). Cohen argues that men heard these appeals too, of course, and in response they came to see *her* orgasm, alongside his, as a measure of successful sex (with simultaneous orgasms being the 'gold standard' or ideal – see Altman, 1984). But as various critics have pointed out, men still tended to place themselves at the epicentre of heterosexual sex (Ehrenreich, 1987; Rubin, 1991). Thus, the woman's orgasm was construed as something that he would 'give' to her, partly *for* her but also as a sign or ratification of his own sexual prowess. And yet, because coitus remained at the very heart of what people understood as sex, men found themselves (and *still* find themselves) in a situation where they are very likely to 'fail'. Once again, we can draw upon the testimonies found in Hite's *Report on Male Sexuality* to illustrate the situation of countless numbers of men who were caught up in this same double bind. Here is just one such example:

> I have never (in the last twenty years) made my partner climax. Many times it is my fault, coming within fifty to seventy-five strokes. Other times I can go for many hundred strokes and she still won't ever be approaching her orgasm. It is probably simply a matter of will power. But if I had a dollar for every time that I have counted numbers or gone over plans in my head, anything to avoid thinking about what I was doing so as to squeeze out ten to twenty more strokes, I would be wealthy.

(Hite, 1990: 356)

THE MEANING OF SEX

It should be clear already that sex is much more than just a physical event or an array of erotic activities. As with all of these different aspects of men's lives, it is the *meaning*, or significance, of sexual practices that makes them so interesting and important. Just as getting a job or becoming a father serve as signal moments in a boy's transition to manhood, so it is with sex. In many cultures around the world, losing one's virginity is seen as a rite of passage, a symbol of having graduated into the community of adults (Carpenter, 2002). Hite's (1990) volume contains a short section which deals with men's accounts of experiencing intercourse for the very first time. As a collection of stories it is a pretty mixed bag. There are tales of wonderment, ecstasy and surprise but also descriptions of embarrassment, bemusement and dismay. Yet common to many of the stories was a sense of relief that the protagonist had finally 'done it' and thus become a man.

As part of her examination of men, Chesler (1978) asked several of her male interviewees if they enjoyed sex. She reported that most were rather taken aback by the question. 'Of course . . . who doesn't?' was the typical kind of response. Such replies tie into a pervasive understanding of sex – or what Plummer (1995) would call a familiar *sexual story*. In this account, men are *driven* to have sex; it is held to be part of their very constitution – even their *raison d'être*.

Here are just a few examples of this kind of sentiment, taken from Hite's mighty compendium:

> Sex just 'is'. We 'are', sex 'is'. It's a drive. Native and all that. The desire to copulate is the ultimate drive among all living things, not only humans.

> My appetite for sex and food are similar: the more you gorge yourself, the more often you must have it!

> To penetrate a vagina is the male's reason of existence. It's a strong, driving force that cannot be lessened except by the act of copulation itself. I think it's the greatest thing on earth, a God-given wonder. Physically, it's driving continually. A male is *always* looking and wanting.

> Men are simple. Men want pussy. Women have it.

As we can see from the last two examples, there is often a strongly **heteronormative** flavour to this way of talking about sex (i.e. something that simply assumes or takes for granted that sexual relations are between men and women), although it is by no means uncommon for gay men to use the same tropes of 'drives' and insatiable 'appetites' (Dowsett, 1996). What is more, the concept of *nature*, or the *natural*, is often at the fore in these accounts. The desire for sex is seen as being outside of the conscious control of men, the urge to procreate as something hardwired into their very DNA. More than any other, it is this way of understanding male sexuality that underpins the coital imperative, for within its terms, vaginal penetration and ejaculation are seen as the 'logical conclusion' of sex (Gavey *et al.*, 1999). This imperative carries with it a number of implications. One thing it means is that all other forms of sexual activity are subordinated, regarded as mere *fore*-play, or just warm-up acts, for the main event. Moreover, the imperative imposes a kind of *grammar* for heterosexual sex: an order of activity which is highly pervasive, predictable and, in many women's estimations, all too perfunctory (Hite, 1990).

> It was like he knew there had to be foreplay – so a couple of squeezes up here, then a quick rummage down there and straight in.
>
> (Duncombe and Marsden, 1996: 227)

Coitus generally exists, therefore, not as just part of the sexual repertoire of heterosexual couples but as its terminal act. More specifically, sex typically ends when, within sexual intercourse, the man ejaculates. As Johnson (2010) explains, if, within sex, a man *hasn't* ejaculated, he is likely to feel one of two things: either that he has 'failed' (as a *man* as much as anything) or that he has yet to finish! Women often know that it is difficult (and sometimes even dangerous) to withdraw from having sex before the man has had an orgasm (Gavey *et al.*, 1999). However, the opposite is seldom true. In other words, whilst women's orgasms may be an aim or aspiration within contemporary hetero-sex, the man's orgasm has a different status: his is seen more as a matter of expectation or *entitlement*, rather than just an option (Braun *et al.*, 2003).

There is no doubt that this way of understanding male sexuality has a good deal of currency in the modern world. However, like those accounts of men losing their virginity, there is more than one tale to tell about the place of sex in men's lives. An alternative *sexual story* is one that emphasises *intimacy* rather than lust. In their article about the coital imperative, Gavey *et al.* make a telling assertion, claiming that: 'men's 'need' for emotional intimacy is possibly one of the open secrets of heterosexuality' (1999: 52). What 'cannot be acknowledged', they say, is the fact that men's desire for intimacy contravenes the assumed *gendering* of sexuality. Common sense, in the West at least, tells us that it is *women* who seek intimacy from sex, whereas men's focus is on 'just getting off' (Johnson, 2010; see also Seidman, 1989). However, Hite's (1990) survey provides us with no little evidence of men quite prepared to divulge this particular 'secret':

> Intercourse with my lover gives me a warm and wanted feeling. It makes me feel valuable to someone.

> It [coitus] is the closest you can be to a person, and for a moment or an hour it overcomes the loneliness and separation of life.

> When we are naked, conversation rarely centers on the weather or trivialities. Emotions are bared and truths are revealed.

> I like the feeling of the sexual contact but also the feeling of someone liking you enough to give their body to you. I appreciate the confirmation I receive. It is a wonderful feeling.

> (325ff)

Back in the 1980s, Wendy Hollway wrote an influential piece about the ways in which heterosexual couples spoke about sex (Hollway, 1984). Alongside what she termed the 'male sex-drive discourse', she identified another way of conceptualising sex: the so-called 'have & hold' discourse. Here sexual relations are referred to not as some kind of animal drive or instinct but as the preserve of stable, long-term relationships. Sex is held here to be an expression of love. It is something that people do not because they've got the urge or the itch but as a way of demonstrating their feelings of commitment and respect. Once again, Hite's work provides us with some pertinent examples of men speaking in these terms:

> Sex is mainly to show how one cares and loves the other; sex is the natural expression of love.

> Why do I like intercourse? Because I love her so.

> An orgasm is a physical and emotional crescendo – a release of withheld expression, things I cannot tell her in any other way.

> Intercourse is an exquisite expression of 'I love you'.
>
> (1990: 327–8)

Of course, the concept of sexual *stories* (Plummer, 1995) brings with it connotations of *fabrication* or *fiction* – stuff that has been 'made up'. We might be inclined to think that, whilst men may be heard sometimes to say these kinds of things, they don't necessarily *mean* them. One might suspect that they 'trot out' these lines to disguise their true carnal nature – or even as a strategy of seduction. However, this is not an interpretation that writers such as Hollway and Plummer would accept. For them (or, perhaps I should say, *us*), these ways of constructing sex are not *mere* talk; rather, they are the very frameworks through which men (and women) both imagine and experience their sexuality. Look, for example, at the following exchange, which comes from one of Hollway's later studies:

Jim   I remember I had a very strong thing for many years that you shouldn't actually sleep with someone unless you were actually in love with them in some way. If you did it

> with someone you weren't in love with, it was somehow pretty horrid and pretty nasty.

Wendy To them?

Jim Well it was just, it showed you weren't – yeah, I suppose it showed the importance of sex. That it was so special that you shouldn't squander it [. . .] I never had casual sex with anyone.

Wendy Was that what you wanted, or was it a moral imperative?

Jim One reason was feeling that sex was kind of dangerous. If you had sex it meant you were committed in some way and I didn't want that. Also that it said something – if you just had sex without a relationship, it was letting them down, 'cos you somehow thought that they'd expect a relationship and it was a pretty shitty thing to do, to have one part of it without the other.

(Hollway, 1989: 62)

Tellingly, whilst Jim offered this account as something that had shaped his past, he did go on to say that it was a feeling that had, to some extent, stayed with him. That is, even though he thought it rather an old-fashioned (or 'prissy') point of view, casual sex still struck him as somewhat immoral. What this demonstrates is that sexual stories can bite! It underlines the argument that there is no specific *truth* of male sexuality, no bedrock of experience either to be discovered or denied. Rather, it shows that the ways that men approach and feel about sex are, in part at least, the *consequences* of the ways that it is storied – not the other way around.

TWISTS IN THE TALES OF SEX

The American author John Gray has made quite a name for himself (and, of course, a fortune) by putting about the idea that men and women are worlds apart in terms of their sexuality (for example, Gray, 1995). However, what academic research tends to show is that, across both time and space, there is a good deal of variability in terms of how people both understand themselves and conduct their lives as sexual beings. For example, Louisa Allen's (2003) research in New Zealand showed that young men and women seemed much less tied to those traditionally gendered scripts in which boys claim to need sex and girls say that they are after love. She found women who described themselves as sexually driven and also men who, like Jim in the previous extract, spoke of sex as just part of a loving relationship. A somewhat similar picture emerges from the work of Maxwell (2007), but this time in a UK context. She found both sexes using a mixture of accounts, including boys talking about the kudos of having a long line of 'conquests' as well as how much they wanted a partner who would 'be there' for them – someone with whom they could be themselves and someone they could trust.

Other research has drawn attention to some of the contextual factors which seem to impinge upon the uptake of these sexual stories. For instance, Eck (2014) suggests that *age* makes a difference. She points out that whilst it is accepted (or even expected) that younger men will see sexual relations as all about scoring notches on bedposts, for middle-aged men the stakes are quite different. For them to engage in such behaviour risks courting censure or ridicule because, she argues, by that stage in a man's life, society would expect him to have 'settled down' with a wife and, in all probability, children. Eck's focus, in this study, was on middle-aged men who were single (either through divorce or having never married), and she found that they faced a difficult dilemma involving a kind of trade-off between masculinity and maturity. The pursuit of new sexual relationships affirmed their manhood but made them appear juvenile, whereas to settle into life as a single man made them seem mature but sexually dysfunctional (i.e. a bit of a 'loser'). Eck reported that, as a way of managing this dilemma, many of the men described themselves as deliberately withdrawing from sex. In other words, they implied that whilst they could easily 'get laid' if they wanted to, playing the field was something that no longer held much appeal. There are some clear parallels between this study and the research of Terry (2012) on men who practised celibacy. As with Eck's respondents, all of Terry's interviewees presented themselves as sexual beings: that is, none of them explained their celibacy in terms of a lack of libido. Indeed, several stressed the rigours of giving up sex: that it was *hard* to resist the impulse or drive for sexual satisfaction. As in Eck's study, these men stressed that they had made a conscious decision to give up sex. It wasn't that they couldn't 'get any'; rather, it was a deliberate policy of withdrawal. At a stroke, therefore, these men were able to present themselves as normal, 'red-blooded' males, whose strength of resolve or willpower was enough to override the dictates of their very carnal nature.

Another, more complicated account of the contextualisation of male sexuality appears in the work of Ray and Rosow (2010). In their study they looked at the ways in which both black and white members of US college fraternities talked about their relationships with women. What they found was a basic disparity: compared to white fraternity members, black college men were more likely to invoke the language of romance, rather than seeing women as merely a source of sexual gratification. What was most interesting about their research, however, was the way that the authors accounted for this patterning. At the heart of their explanation was the fact that black fraternity members were very much in the minority. As such, compared to their white counterparts, they seemed to feel more responsible for their behaviour around women, sensing that, if they were disrespectful, then it might bring shame upon their group as a whole. Another factor considered by Ray and Rosow was the physical accommodation of the two sets of students. They pointed out that whilst white students were often located in large fraternity houses, black students were more likely to live off campus, in smaller, rented flats. What this meant was that white students had, quite literally, less space for romance in their lives. As one (white) student explained:

> Frat houses aren't the place for [romantic behaviour] . . . the place is filthy and you have no privacy. None. I shower with five guys; people always coming in and out. You're never alone. I used to feel weird about it [sex], but now I don't. Like I used to try to be quiet, but I'm having sex less than four feet from my roommate, who's having sex with his girlfriend. You're going to hear something. So you don't worry about it.
>
> (Ray and Rosow, 2010: 538)

Of course, what no longer 'worries' him is being heard having sex; to be heard *making love* might be an entirely different matter. In such an environment, that would probably remain a taboo, as it renders the young men open to the charge of being 'soft', enthralled or, in the lingo of US college culture, 'pussy-whipped' (see also Gilmartin, 2007).

In another US-based project looking at the intersection of sexuality, ethnicity and class, Carissa Froyum (2007) considered the situation of black teenagers from low-income families. She claimed that, in the face of this dual disadvantage, such youngsters become highly invested in what remains for them in terms of the main axes of identity, with *heterosexuality* carrying much of the burden of their need for self-esteem. She notes that anti-gay or homophobic sentiments were a common feature of her interviews with members of this group, with homosexual lifestyles being castigated as unnatural and immoral. Of particular interest was their tendency to see homosexuality as a matter of individual *choice*. There was much talk of people 'going gay', or being drawn into homosexuality, rather than it being something outside of a person's control. As Froyum points out, this not only allowed her respondents to present gays and lesbians as morally culpable (and deserving, therefore, of whatever opprobrium came their way), but it also served to underline their own superiority in having chosen the 'right' path.

Throughout the years, there have been many studies that have highlighted the role played by homophobia in the formation and maintenance of masculine identities – particularly within the lives of adolescents (for example, Lehne, 1998; Kimmel, 2001; Frosh *et al.*, 2002). For those with a leaning towards psychoanalytic explanations, homophobia is seen to have its roots deep within the male psyche, as a means of trying to deny or suppress anxieties about their own homosexual desires (Messner, 2010). Others, however, have suggested that homophobia operates at the level of social interaction, as a routine method by which people present themselves as straight (Nayak and Kahily, 1996; Edley, 2006). In a much cited paper, Pascoe (2005) claimed that whilst taunts such as 'gay' and 'fag' are a ubiquitous feature of adolescent culture, they are often barely related to matters of sexuality (see also Stoudt, 2006). Someone might get called a 'fag' for dropping an easy catch, saying something stupid or tripping on a kerb. Equally, the epithet 'gay' can be applied not just to people but to inanimate objects such as mobile phones, films and clothing. Of course, it is not insignificant that synonyms of homosexuality should become generalised insults, but it does force us to think again about the status of such terms. Some (like Pascoe) see homophobia as a means of staking a claim to masculinity (where a 'fag' fails to display the requisite courage, control, composure, etc.). Froyum (2007), on the other hand, turns that relationship upside down. In her eyes, acting like a 'real' man (or indeed a 'real' woman) is a key way of demonstrating one's heterosexuality. She claims, in other words, that gender is something pressed into the service of cementing sexual identities, not the other way around.

GAY MASCULINITIES

There is a telling moment in Pascoe's (2005) study, when one of his interviewees claimed that whilst he often made liberal use of the ritual insults 'fag' and 'gay', he would never use them to 'call out' someone who was themselves gay; that, he implied, would be beyond the pale. Another boy added: 'Being gay is just a lifestyle. It's someone you choose to sleep with. You can still throw around a football and be gay' (337). It is interesting to hear, in these comments, the dislocation of masculinity and sexuality, not least because it would appear to be a relatively new phenomenon. Indeed, some would see it as marking the beginnings of an unravelling of a form of common sense that has been part of Western culture for almost 150 years.

In *The History of Sexuality*, Michel Foucault (1979) makes a striking assertion: that homosexuality came into being in 1870. Of course, he wasn't trying to suggest that prior to that date there had been no sexual contact between people of the same sex. He knew very well that, in centuries gone by, there were laws in countries such as England and France which strictly forbade acts of *sodomy*. Foucault's point was that prior to 1870 such acts were seen as sins that *anybody* might commit (in the same way that anyone might commit adultery or steal from a neighbour). Foucault argued that this way of thinking was radically transformed in the late nineteenth century, through the work of the early 'sexologists', such as Sigmund Freud, Havelock Ellis and Richard von Krafft-Ebing. Together, they put forward the argument that such acts should be considered not so much as crimes but as the signs of *mental illness*. The shift was not just a change in jurisdiction, from the magistrate to the psychiatrist; the most significant difference was that homosexual acts were now regarded as indicative of a particular *kind of person*. Over the course of the next few decades, these same sexologists sought to produce a detailed portrait of the homosexual. Amongst other things, they argued that he was characterized by a particular kind of body shape, a dislike of children and, most bizarrely of all, an inability to whistle! According to their reckoning:

> Nothing that went into his total composition was unaffected by his sexuality. It was everywhere present in him: at the root of all his actions.
>
> (Foucault, 1979: 43)

It was Krafft-Ebing who would go on to suggest that homosexuals were gender *inverts*: that is, women trapped inside the bodies of men (Weeks, 1986). The publicity surrounding the trial of Oscar Wilde (in 1895) would also help to cement in the public mind an image of the homosexual as an effeminate individual, lacking the hallmarks of true masculinity. Rather than sturdy and stoical, the gay man was seen as timid, effusive and ineffectual. Of course, much has changed over the intervening years – although not without a struggle (Altman, 1972). Alongside the rise of second wave feminism came the emergence of Gay Liberation, a movement dedicated to challenging the way that gay men and lesbians were treated both by the state and within civil society. A number of landmark victories ensued; for instance, the UK began the process of decriminalising homosexuality in 1967 and, seven years later, the American Psychological Association (APA) struck homosexuality from its official list of psychological disorders. Nevertheless, as Humphries (1985) explains, many gay men growing up around this time harboured a strong sense of themselves as being *less* than a proper man. Living within a (patriarchal) culture that always valued male over female, they were thought of as 'sissies', 'pansies' and 'wimps'.

In a section on gay sexuality, Hite (1990) expresses her dislike of the term 'homosexuality': she calls it an 'anti-word'. What she means is that homosexuality appears as a negative identity: a case of *not being* 'straight'. However, as I explained in Chapter 2, some gender theorists see the symbolic (and *psychological*) relationship as running in the opposite direction. Object Relations theorists see masculinity as a form of *not being* like a woman (i.e. the 'flight from the feminine'), and in Connell's (1995) account of the gender order, *hegemonic masculinity* is said to be held in place through a whole series of oppositions, including a contrast with gay men. Furthermore, in the broader literature, it is not difficult to find autobiographical accounts from men who talk about life growing up as a near constant struggle *not* to appear as either effeminate or gay (for example, Jackson, 1990; Messner, 2010). It is highly significant, therefore, that the writings of so many gay and so-called *queer theorists* are dedicated to disrupting these symbolic associations (Butler, 1990; Halberstam, 1998). For example, Humphries (1985) wrote about the rise of *gay machismo*, which involved gay men adopting formerly straight codes of appearance (for example, leather, denim, 'bovver' boots and moustaches). As with feminism, there was both a personal and a political side to these actions. First, they pressed the point that gay men weren't necessarily 'camp' or effete – that they too can be tough and assertive – even aggressive. They emphasised the fact that, erotically speaking, gay men are often drawn to masculine types (as is true, of course, of many heterosexual women) and also that gay relationships don't have to echo the conventions of hetero-sex. They showed that, in many cases, they weren't a union of opposites but a celebration of *sameness* – and, as such, more likely to be characterised by equality rather than relations of domination (Weeks *et al.*, 2001).

Yet queer theorists have done much more than merely upset the equation of gay men and effeminacy. Indeed, they have sought to trouble the very distinction between gay and straight. Over the years, there have been many attempts by governments and other agencies to find out what proportion of people in a given population are gay, straight or bisexual. They usually do this by survey, asking people just to indicate their sexual orientation. Generally speaking, the numbers identifying as gay are fairly small (for example, just over 1 per cent in the 2015 ONS poll of Britons). However, there are good reasons to be sceptical about such figures. Back in the late 1940s, the sexologist Alfred Kinsey published the first of two large-scale surveys on the sex lives of the American public (Kinsey *et al.*, 1948). Instead of asking people to categorise themselves, he enquired into the details of their sexual experiences. For example, he asked men if they had ever had sexual contact with another man, to the point of achieving an orgasm. Much to the astonishment of US society, over one third reported that they had. On the basis of his overall findings, Kinsey claimed that, roughly speaking, 30 per cent of the US population was exclusively straight, 10 per cent exclusively gay and the rest somewhere in between. Does that mean, therefore, that lots of people lie when they report their sexual orientation, or are millions of people somehow living in denial? In truth, it is probably neither of these things. Instead, it more likely reflects how we *theorise* sexuality. Asking somebody if they are gay, straight or bisexual presumes not only that sexuality is categorical, but also that it is something that remains stable over time. On both counts, queer theorists would often beg to differ. In their estimations, human sexuality is not something that is set in stone (or even flesh and blood!); rather, it is something much more fluid and contingent.

In the masculinities literature, some writers have taken to using the acronym MSM, which stands for 'Men who have Sex with Men' – instead of 'gay' or 'homosexual' (for example, Goode-Cross and Good, 2008). It reflects a growing opinion that sexual *practices* have an uneasy fit with sexual *identities*. Of course, it would be quite wrong to suggest that academics have only just recognised the potential for a mismatch between what people do and how they think of themselves sexually. Almost as far back as Kinsey, Albert Reiss was writing about how young male prostitutes maintained heterosexual identities in the face of their encounters with male clients (Reiss, 1961; see also Özbay, 2010). Often through the testimonies of sex workers, academics have long known that many men enjoy sexual relations with other men whilst thinking of themselves as entirely heterosexual (there are several such examples in Hite's *Report* on men). Rather, what appears to be relatively new is the diminishing currency of the 'standard' sexual identities themselves. Seidman *et al.* (1999) have argued that, ironically, gay identities (and indeed gay culture) are receding from view as they become more mainstream (see also Bech, 2003). Similarly, Anderson (2009) argues that, within the US, the signs of homophobia are very much on the retreat, especially amongst the younger generations. Even within the ranks of college sportsmen, who have so often been at the very epicentre of hegemonic masculinity, he found evidence of a level of homosocial contact and intimacy that, in such circumstances, would have been almost inconceivable 30 years ago (Anderson and McCormack, 2015). The media are awash with stories about the rise of gender 'fluidity' and the emergence of new sexual identities, such as **pan-** and **polysexual**. In one much publicised nationwide survey (YouGov, 2015), it was claimed that only half of British young adults (aged 18–24) now see themselves as straight. Heasley (2005) has suggested that the *queering* of straight masculinities takes a number of different forms, from incorporating aspects of gay culture and taking a stand against homophobic slurs to more passive forms of resistance, like just not joining in as being 'one of the lads'.

Needless to say, it would be a mistake to imagine that these developments are taking place uniformly, right across the globe. In reality, the picture is much more complicated. There are locations where the weakening of heteronormativity seems to be only just under way and others where its progress is more obvious but patchy. Guasch (2011) reports, for example, that there is a growing acceptance of both gay lifestyles and gay culture in the metropolitan parts of Spain but not in the more rural areas. In other regions (for example, across large tracts of Africa, Asia and the Middle East) there are no signs of any such transformations. Indeed, in places like Afghanistan, Nigeria and Saudi Arabia, homosexual acts can result in criminalisation, imprisonment and even the death penalty. And lest we fall into feeling rather smug about the situation that pertains in places such as the UK and the US, it is worth remembering this: on 12 June, 2016, during the writing of this very chapter, 49 innocent people were murdered in a gun attack on a gay nightclub in Orlando, Florida. It (almost) goes without saying that the killer was a man.

FURTHER READING

Allen, L. (2003) 'Girls Want Sex, Boys Want Love: Resisting dominant discourses of (hetero) sexuality'. *Sexualities*, 6(2): 215–36.
This is an interesting article, which looks at how young adults talk about sexual relations in ways that contravene the standard 'sexual stories' of men as active pursuers of sex and women as passive 'gatekeepers'.

Duncombe, J. and Marsden, D. (1996) 'Whose Orgasm Is This Anyway? "Sex work" in long-term heterosexual couple relationships'. In J. Weeks and J. Holland (eds) *Sexual Cultures: Communities, Values and Intimacy*. London: Macmillan (220–38).
This is a fascinating, if somewhat depressing, article about the trajectories of heterosexual relations between established couples. Twenty years on, it remains as relevant as ever.

Hite, S. (1990) *The Hite Report on Male Sexuality*. London: Optima.
I have made liberal use of this resource – but it has so much more to offer. It is a veritable treasure trove of information about (American) men's attitudes, feelings and practices around sex. Hite's *Report* is a unique body of work.

Potts, A. (2000) '"The Essence of the Hard-On": Hegemonic masculinity and the cultural construction of "erectile dysfunction"'. *Men and Masculinities*, 3(1): 85–103.
This article looks at how what was once considered a natural aspect of men's aging is now regarded as a medical condition requiring active intervention – a study, therefore, of both the social construction of infirmity and the politics of the penis!

Weeks, J. (2016) *Sexuality* (4th. edition). London: Routledge.
This is a truly remarkable little book – now in its fourth edition. In clear, authoritative prose, Weeks explains that sexuality is far from being an expression of natural urges or instincts. Rather, he shows it to be something that is intensely cultural, historical and political.

7

MALE VIOLENCE

> Women may get angry, threaten and scream, lash out in fury or seek murder and revenge [but] only men habitually prey on those weaker than themselves, stalk the night in search of the lonely victim, hunt one another in packs, devise initiation rituals, exquisite tortures, extermination camps, delight in 'Russian Roulette' . . . and all the world's never-ending games of fear, pain and death.
>
> (Miles, 1992: 15)

As this book plainly demonstrates, academic studies of men and masculinity are sites and sources of tremendous controversy. Irrespective of whether the focus is upon men's sexuality, parenting, their place in the economy (and so on), one is usually faced with a cacophony of voices offering all kinds of different opinion. However, if there is just one small island of consensus within this great sea of contention, it would be the suggestion that men are more violent than women. As Rosalind Miles points out in the quotation above, women are not incapable of acting violently (indeed, two minutes spent on the internet can reveal a whole host of sites dedicated to female serial killers, such as Aileen Wuornos and Myra Hindley), but, as I indicated at the very start of the book, we don't readily associate women with acts of murder, torture and rape (hence the public – and academic – fascination with those women who do). In the case of men, such behaviours somehow seem much less remarkable. In the course of her examination of men, Miles (1992) draws upon a quote from the British psychotherapist Phillip Hodson, who noted that, during the twentieth century alone, over 50 million people died at the hands of 'psychiatrically normal males'. Men are, he said, 'the death sex'.

As one might anticipate, there has been a concerted lobby of theorists and activists who have pushed the idea that men are (more) violent by *nature*. A strange alliance of radical feminists, ethologists and evolutionary psychologists have argued that violence is hard-wired into men's very being: that they cannot help but wreak misery and suffering upon the world. Fingers have been pointed towards various sites of the male body as the main source of the problem: the 'warrior' gene, the '**dimorphic' brain** and, of course, the male sex hormone, testosterone. Yet none of these (reductive) explanations do justice to the real complexities of male violence (Turner, 1994). As Gilbert (1994: 352) observes, male violence may well 'outrank disease and famine as the major source of human suffering', but it is by no means an inevitable consequence of men's organic or material design. Whilst ubiquitous, male violence is far from universal. There are communities and cultures dotted around the world where violence doesn't really feature (such as amongst the Amish) and, where it does occur, the rates of incidence vary tremendously from one place to the next (Gilligan, 2010). Moreover, as Connell (2000) points out, we must always remember that whilst the vast majority of killers are male, such men are far outnumbered by those who do not kill, rape or commit acts of common assault.

In this final chapter, I want to look in more detail at these arguments. As will become clear, whilst there may be a broad consensus around the idea that men are the more violent sex, it is not due to the existence of a simple or obvious explanation. Part of the complexity comes out of the fact that male violence is mul-tifaceted. For example, Archer (1994a) claims that the dynamics vary according to the character of the victim. In the pages that follow, therefore, we will be looking at different aspects of male violence, including domestic violence, sexual violence and men's violation of each other. I also want to consider the significance of both militarism and war. But before we proceed any further, it is worth spending a moment to offer a bit of conceptual clarification. In the introduction to Archer's (1994a) edited volume, he notes that, across the social sciences, there has been a general tendency to conflate considerations of male violence with those of *aggression*. Yet, as he points out, these things are not synonymous. Aggression is a much broader concept. We talk about things like aggressive *music* and aggressive *trading* – one can even use the term to describe a way of playing chess! For Archer, violence is a type of activity which involves not just a display of forcefulness but the infliction of either physical or psychological damage, destruction and/or harm. It is this definition that will provide the main focus of this chapter.

MARTIAL MASCULINITY

If we look again at the quotation from Miles, we might recognise that of all the 'never-ending games of fear, pain and death', one of the most devastating is war. This is an issue that has both vexed and divided gender theorists. Across the field as a whole, it has been seen as offering an image of all that is bad *and* good about men and masculinity. Hodson would certainly see war as a damning indictment of the male sex, given that a high proportion of those 50 million deaths would have occurred within the context of battle. Yet one could easily argue that Hodson was making rather expedient use of those statistics in his (rather startling) assessment of men and masculinity. One might point to the fact that in countries all around the world, women have been prevented from joining the armed forces, at least in combat roles (although even here, as elsewhere, there are signs that things are starting to change[1] – see Higate and Hopton, 2005) and suggest that were it not for these prohibitions, women would have just as much blood on their hands. Nevertheless, there are a number of gender theorists who take a very different line in maintaining that war is both a consequence and, in a sense, a celebration of masculinity (Harstock, 1989). So when, for example, President George W. Bush announced America's 'War on Terror', in 2001, it would have been seen by some as the launch of an inherently masculinist initiative or campaign. In their eyes, it was an almost classic illustration of men's brinkmanship and brutality.

There is, though, a third position in these debates. This one holds that there is an intimate relationship between masculinity and war, but it disputes the direction of influence. In a nutshell, the argument is that war makes men, rather than the other way around. In other words, the claim is that masculinity is a result or consequence of men's (or boys') exposure, either to war itself or to a culture that champions what McCarthy (1994) calls 'warrior values'. Now, of course, it seems rather peculiar to think of violence as something that society might aim to promote or encourage, but there is no shortage of evidence to support that thesis. In Chapter 3, we heard how, in ancient Greece and in nineteenth-century England, men were encouraged to harden their bodies, in readiness to spring to the defence of the state. But in order to create an effective fighting force, one needs more than bulging muscles; one needs an appropriate 'frame of mind'. In his work, McCarthy (1994) describes how, from the Sambia tribe of New Guinea and the Massai of East Africa, through to the Samurai code in Japan and even the Mafia in present-day Sicily, many cultures have heaped great honour and status upon their fighting heroes. He explains how, in some parts of the world, proving oneself as a warrior is a prerequisite for obtaining wealth, authority and, in some cases, even a wife. Moreover, in all of these cultures, it isn't just a case of waiting to see which individuals reveal these characteristics and then plying them with rewards; rather, attempts are made to *instil* these warrior values.

In the Western world, the promotion of martial masculinity has been effected by various institutions. As Higate and Hopton (2005) point out, organisations like the Scouts and Boys' Brigade have played an important role in countries like the UK and the US (Mangan and Walvin, 1987). The UK also has what is known as the Combined Cadet Force (CCF), sponsored by the Ministry of Defence, which has introduced generations of young boys (and, more recently, girls, too) to aspects of militarism, including how to use a gun. Higate and Hopton (2005) also draw attention to the influence that popular culture has had in the dissemination of these same values. They note how, during the second half of the twentieth century, comics such as *The Victor* and *The Valiant* sought to inspire young boys with their tales of derring-do and self-sacrifice. They also remark on the impact of television series such as the *A-Team, Magnum PI* and *Airwolf*, where most of the leading characters were seen to come from a military background. It is very easy, of course, to add further to this list of well known 'soldier heroes' (Dawson, 1994) through films such as *Rambo, The Expendables* and *G.I. Joe*.

Whilst it might be tempting to try to resolve the question of whether men make war or wars make men, there are those who would argue that it trades on a false distinction. Hutchings (2008) claims, for example, that there is a reciprocal relationship between masculinity and war, where each serves to sustain and legitimate the other (see also Higate and Hopton, 2005). What they mean, in other words, is that wars need men for their successful prosecution – but at the very same time, men also need things like wars as a means of demonstrating that they are made of what the novelist Tom Wolfe called the 'right stuff' (Wolfe, 1979).

We can begin to see something of these dynamics in the shape of Frank Barrett's study of the US Navy (Barrett, 2001). What he found there was an extraordinarily hierarchical organisation in which men engaged in a near-constant struggle to maximise and then defend their position within the overall pecking order. At the top of the pile were the so-called 'airedales', or aviators – the men who flew jet planes from the Navy's aircraft carriers. Barrett described them as coming closest to the hegemonic ideal: confident, daring and cool under pressure. What's more, he also reported that they had a reputation for being wild and arrogant, excessive in their abuse of both alcohol and women. There were other pilots on the ship as well, such as those who flew helicopters, but, tellingly, they were often derided by the 'airedales' as 'wimps'. Barrett also studied the men who worked in a supporting capacity, as supply officers. Lower still in the hierarchy, these men were derided by those in combat roles as 'supply pussies' or 'suppo-weenies'. Once again, the language used is highly significant: those few that make the grade (i.e. the ones that show they have the 'right stuff') get to call themselves men; but everybody else – the ones who miss the cut – are denied that precious mantle. They are castigated as less-than-men – as homosexuals, women and children. Of course, such taunts were not lost on those who worked below deck; indeed, they lived with those ritual humiliations. Barrett claimed that, to varying degrees, most seemed to accept the status quo, regarding the superiority of the aviators as legitimate. Others seemed not only more resentful but also somewhat keener to 'talk up' the importance of their own role within the force.

In the course of his analysis, Barrett noted that, following Janowitz (1960), military men can be regarded as 'professionals in violence'. It is a designation that carries with it a number of important implications. First of all, it points to the fact that such men are *specialists* in the perpetration of violence – that they have been trained to do it efficiently and effectively. Second, it indicates that the state endorses those actions – that they are regarded as both valuable and legitimate. Another implication, of course, is that such men are sober and responsible in the deployment of their fighting skills. As McCarthy (1994) makes plain, the true warrior is honourable as well as deadly. There are rules of engagement, even in war, and a 'professional' prides himself on abiding by those rules. In reality, however, things are nothing like so neat and tidy. Within the masculinities literature concerns have been expressed about the excessive nature of martial masculinity (for example, Enloe, 2004): about its tendency to spill over with disastrous effects, whether within theatres of war, military establishments (such as the Deepcut Army Barracks in England) or civilian life.

Before we move on to a different debate, I think it is worthwhile drawing attention to the connections that exist between martial masculinity and sport. Over the years, many have pointed to the parallels between the two domains; for example, Williams (1985) notes that the metaphors of war and sport are thoroughly intertwined. Looking back at Chapter 3, we should now see more clearly how sports have provided a thoroughgoing apprenticeship in the inculcation of warrior values, including a preparedness to sacrifice oneself for the sake of the team. Certainly, sport can be held up as another area of life in which violence is encouraged. Boxing is probably the epitome of that ideology, where the greatest honour goes not to those with the highest levels of skill but to those with either the most destructive punch or most resilient chin. In contact sports like rugby, American football and ice hockey, a premium is placed upon the ability, and willingness, to inflict big 'hits' upon one's opponents. Obviously, as with war, there are supposed to be limits to the degree of violence used in sport. Indeed, for writers such as Norbert Elias and Eric Dunning, sport is valued precisely as a mechanism for civilising or curbing what they see as the worst excesses of human nature (Dunning, 1999). But many of those working within the field of men and masculinities would simply disagree; in their estimations, the culture of sport, like the culture of the military, is a recipe for all manner of abuses – against teammates, opponents and others, off as well as on the field of play (Benedict and Klein, 1997; Curry, 2000; Messner, 1990).

GENDERED VIOLENCE

As we have now seen, some theorists believe that violence is, in essence, a masculine mode of engagement with the world. Ahmad and Smith (1994) have suggested, for instance, that where boys might vent their frustrations through the use of violence, girls will tend to use other means, such as malicious gossip and ostracism. Others have argued that both sexes can act violently, albeit in distinctly gendered ways. For example, Campbell and Muncer (1994) stress that whilst there is little difference between men and women in terms of the frequency of and propensity to experience negative emotions like frustration and anger, the violence that tends to ensue has a very different character and logic. Drawing upon an established (and, some might say, rather dusty or discredited) sociological distinction, they argue that male violence is *instrumental*, whilst women's tends to be more *expressive*. In an effort to illustrate (and corroborate) this argument, they looked at how different people talk about their experiences of acting violently. The quotes from the male protagonists were all about standing up for themselves, not backing down and showing the world they meant business. The woman's account, by contrast, was a tale of blind fury. She described herself as thrashing around, kicking and screaming, utterly out of control. The differences between the accounts were palpable: echoing the quotation from Miles, women certainly appear to get mad, but there seems to be something a good deal more calculated or *strategic* about men's use of violence. That said, we do need to be a little bit careful in taking such accounts at face value. As many a lawyer knows, stories of untrammelled rage have often being used in attempts to mitigate blame for all kinds of crimes and misdemeanours. Likewise, when men talk, in a matter-of-fact way, about 'sorting somebody out' or 'putting them in their place', they aren't necessarily giving us a neutral account of what happened. As Butler (1990) pointed out, people are often *doing* or 'performing' as gendered beings in the telling of themselves and of their actions (see also West and Zimmerman, 1987).

Irrespective of such considerations, it is very hard to dispute the suggestion that there are significant gender differences in terms of the sheer scale and scope of violence in modern life. As we have heard, societies can encourage violence in particular domains but, for the most part, it is something both frowned upon and, in its more excessive forms, legislated against. Therefore, we can look at crime statistics as a source of information about the gendering of violence. What those statistics offer is a very clear picture: in almost every part of the world, men are much more likely than women to commit violent crimes. Given that the more serious offences (such as robbery, assault and murder) usually result in custodial sentences, then prison populations can serve as a reasonable proxy. In the UK today, for example, approximately 95 per cent of the prison population is male – a figure that is more or less repeated in countries all over the Western world (see the *International Centre for Prison Studies* – www.prisonstudies.org). Yet if we dig a bit deeper into these statistics, we soon discover that the perpetrators of violent crimes are not uniformly distributed across any given population of men. Rather, violent crime has a certain set of demographics, which can help us in shedding further light on the gendering of violence. One clear pattern is that *younger* men are more likely to be found guilty of these kinds of crime, particularly within the age bracket of 14–25 years. Another trend follows socio-economic factors, with a disproportionate number of offenders coming from lower-class strata. A third factor is ethnicity. In countries like the UK and the US, black men are about five times more likely than whites to find themselves behind bars (there is, of course, a significant overlap or interrelationship between ethnicity and socio-economics – see Messerschmidt, 1997).

In an effort to understand how these different factors work together, I would like to look at one of the most extraordinary and, it must be said, outrageous instances of male violence – namely, US school (and/or college) shootings. Research shows that these tragic events are by no means a new or contemporary phenomenon; indeed, there are records of such incidents going back well over 200 years. Nevertheless, public concerns have certainly been raised in recent years, following a spate of particularly bloody killings. Since the Columbine High School massacre in 1999, there have been no less than six similar incidents, which, in total, have accounted for the lives of over one hundred innocent victims. Moreover, in all but one of these attacks, the atrocities ended with the assailant turning their gun on themselves. In examining these events, Eric Madfis (2014) identifies a surprising fact: contrary to the predominant patterns of male violence (as briefly outlined above), this particular form of crime is typically perpetrated by those from the more privileged sections of society. Indeed, following the feminist commentator Gloria Steinem, he refers to them as a 'supremacy crime'. How can we make sense of this anomaly? Why, of all of the different categories of homicide, should this one buck the usual trends? Madfis points out that homicide rates in the US generally follow the ups and downs of the nation's economy. For example, there was a conspicuous rise in the number of people murdered in the 1920s and 30s, during the time of the Great Depression. However, he explains that, over the same period, the incidence of these mass killings didn't spike. Throughout these difficult times, he says, white, middle-class America remained confident that things would turn out all right – that through con-tinued hard work they would end up being rewarded with a better quality of life. And, of course, in the years following the Second World War, that confidence seemed well placed, with living stan-dards rising steadily through the 1950s and 60s. But Madfis argues that everything changed during the 1970s, with the collapse of the US's manufacturing industries and the emergence of a new, globa-lised model of trading relations (see Chapter 4). All of a sudden, some of the more privileged sections of US society felt as if the rug had been pulled from under their feet. The *American dream*, he said, was turning into a nightmare.

> [d]ownward mobility is not merely a matter of accepting a minimal job, enduring the loss of stability, or witnessing with dismay the evaporation of one's hold on material comfort; it is also a broken covenant . . . It is so profound a reversal of middle class

expectations that it calls into question the assumptions upon which their lives have been predicated.

(Newman, 1988: 230, cited in Madfis, 2014)

Madfis claims that the more affluent, white, middle classes lacked the psychological resources to deal with such a setback. Unlike the working classes, they were not inured to the disappointments and privations of life under capitalism. They were left with a sense of shock, bewilderment and betrayal – which, in the case of a few individuals, resulted in a deep determination to seek revenge.

To this point, Madfis has shown us the way in which ethnicity and class combined to create this incendiary context; it is the consideration of gender which helps to complete the picture of why only certain individuals responded in so outrageous a fashion. In explaining this part of the jigsaw, he draws upon an earlier study by the sociologist Jessie Klein (2006). Klein's focus was on the cultural environments of US high schools – and what she found was a scene of intense competition. Now, in the West, of course, schools and colleges are designed to be competitive. They are set up to vie with one another for academic (and sporting) kudos, and they also encourage internal competition amongst the student body for various accolades and awards. However, Klein identified a whole other order of competition in these institutions, aside from those more formal structures. In no small way, the contest amongst the boys was about masculinity, or, more specifically, the desire to be seen as manly. Strikingly similar to Barrett's (2001) findings regarding the culture of the US Navy, Klein found a clear hierarchy operating in the schools. It wasn't the brightest or most academic boys who enjoyed the highest status. Indeed, in the 'masculinity stakes', getting good grades could be positively counterproductive (Willis, 1977). Rather, at the top of the pile were the star athletes, or 'jocks' (see also Edley and Wetherell, 1997). Success with the girls (i.e. sexual 'conquests' of one kind or another) was also a means of garnering the respect of one's peers – albeit far from an independent one, given that the 'jocks' were often the most popular targets for the girls' affections. As noted in the previous chapter, the whole environment was pervaded and policed by a culture of taunting and bullying, with terms like 'fag', 'wimp' and 'nerd' used as ritual insults (Stoudt, 2006). Klein insisted that we need to understand the phenomenon of school shootings within this particular context. Looking at twelve mass shootings, spanning the years 1996 to 2002, she noted that the assailants were seldom the winners in this hegemonic system. In fact, they were usually towards the bottom of the hierarchy. In terms of their physique, they were a long way from what was considered to be ideal; they were often short, fat or scrawny. Many had felt the sting of rejection with respect to girls, their peers and sometimes even members of their own families. It is hardly a coincidence, Klein notes, that many of those critical voices came from individuals who would end up being victims of the shootings.

It is through analyses such as these that we can begin to make sense of the complex interplay of factors that can combine to produce acts of catastrophic violence. We can see that mass shootings, whilst rare, are just not the maverick actions of deranged individuals. There are patterns to these events. Economics plays a role, ethnicity too – and, of course, gender is another vital part of the mix. However, incidents of violence do not always follow from these structures in a straightforward fashion. Violence may well be more prevalent in working-class cultures; it may be rife within black communities; it may be a sign or symbol of masculinity – but it doesn't always mean that the most dangerous individuals are (young) black, working-class men. As shown by Madfis's study, the dynamics can be much more nuanced. In those more recent school shootings, it wasn't a 'triple whammy' of disadvantage that lay behind the murders but a mixture of privilege and humiliation.

GENDERED VICTIMS

It is well documented that women are generally more anxious than men about the prospects of falling victim to a violent attack (Hollander, 2001). However, the reality is that men are the more likely targets. Indeed, the research suggests that the demographic profile of the most vulnerable is virtually identical to that of the main perpetrators; in other words, the victims of violence are most likely young, black and poor (Daly and Wilson, 1994). Hollander (2001) claims that the disparities between the levels of real and imagined risk stem from a highly polarised view of the relationship between gender and violence. Put simply, her argument is that men are seen as the source of all threat (and yet, of themselves, impervious to its dangers), whereas women are cast as the polar opposites – that is, benign or ineffective with respect of their own capacities to harm but also defenceless against any incoming attack (see also Anderson and Umberson, 2001). Hollander conducted a series of focus-group meetings in which she heard no shortage of anxiety expressed about the threat of violence, but she noticed that those concerns were much more likely to be about *women's* (in)security. Time and again, men would speak about themselves as untroubled by worries for their own personal safety. What did give them pause for thought was the vulnerability of their loved ones. Hollander's findings are further supported by a study from Angela Stroud (2012), which looked at (US) men's accounts of why they armed themselves with handguns. She reports that, repeatedly, men would try to justify their actions in terms of being able to protect their wives and children against an attack. Again, relatively few spoke of the weapon as important for their own protection; indeed, many seemed to think that they could 'take care of themselves' without a gun. However, Stroud points to an interesting paradox: in the course of the discussions, many of the men admitted that they were often away from their families. In terms of their own logic, therefore, it would seem to have made more sense that their *wives* (or partners) should take possession of the firearm (Stroud reports that many Americans see such weapons as 'equalizers' – in levelling the destructive capacities of potential victims and their assailants). Yet she found that her male respondents seemed very reluctant to let go of their guns. Stroud reasoned that this was not a reflection of any underlying anxieties about their own safety but more an attachment to the guns' *symbolic* value. More specifically, she claimed that the weapons allow such men to indulge in a fantasy of being latter-day 'frontiersman' – heroic defenders, not just of their own families but also the values of freedom and justice (see also Melzer, 2009).

In his edited collection, John Archer contributes a chapter dedicated to the topic of male-on-male violence (Archer, 1994b). He confirms much of what we've already heard regarding the demographic patterns: that violence is most likely to occur amongst young men living in socially deprived, urban areas. He explains how the highest levels are found amongst those who, in his words, sit 'outside the mainstream institutions of paid employment and marriage' (Archer, 1994b: 125). Indeed, he reports on an earlier study which found that unemployed men were four times more likely than those in work to be involved in an act of homicide (either as perpetrator or victim)! As we saw in the case of school shootings, the reasons behind these patterns can be complicated; but within the mix of precipitating factors, a lack of social integration (and the sense of investment that tends to go with it) seems to be a crucial element. Another contributing factor concerns social attitudes. Research has shown that, from a very young age, people tend to believe that violence aimed at males is less of an issue than that targeted at women or girls (Lombard, 2008). It is assumed, somehow, that men are more able to 'take' it – and in a very real sense they *do*; as Archer (1994b) explains, men and boys are much more likely than women and girls to use 'roughhouse' behaviour in their dealings with one another.

In the same chapter, Archer also talks about an early study by Marvin Wolfgang, who looked into the circumstances which led up to one man killing another (Wolfgang, 1958). He discovered that the initial provocation was often trivial. It could be an off-the-cuff comment or the spilling of someone's beer; in one case, a man stabbed an old friend over a game of dominoes! Wolfgang found that such disputes can escalate very quickly to a point where lives are destroyed. Yet, as Archer explains, these deaths were never really about the loss of a game or a stained shirt; they were about *status* and a sense of masculine pride. It might start with an argument over a parking space. One man gets out of his car and starts shouting and pointing fingers; the other must choose either to sit there and take the abuse or to step out of his own car and confront his accuser – *man to man*. By taking the latter option he sets in train a dangerous game of brinkmanship; neither wants to incur the loss of face involved in backing down but, in a situation such as this, there can only be one 'winner' (even if, by this point, another parking space has become available, this may not defuse the argument – because *that parking space* is the only one that matters). And so the trap is set . . .

In another chapter from the same volume, Archer (1994c) claims that whilst status issues are often at the forefront of male-on-male violence, a different set of dynamics is often used to explain men's violation of women. He claims that violence between men is generally understood as a battle amongst equals for a place within the pecking order. Violence between men and women, on the other hand, is more often seen as a *structural* phenomenon: that is, the product of a patriarchal system. As we heard in Chapter 2, patriarchal societies are ones that give men significant power and control over women's lives – including the 'rights' to punish them. As Archer makes clear, throughout history and across various parts of the world, such societies have condoned violence against women – particularly within the setting of the family. He notes:

> Christianity incorporated this view of the legitimacy of the power of husbands over their wives, and in Europe both church and state maintained it through the centuries. Likewise, wife-beating was accepted as an appropriate way of enforcing such power. In several European countries, the law specified the ways in which the husband could 'chastise' his wife. Adultery was widely viewed as justifying severe violence, even murder; in France it was considered legitimate for a husband to break the nose of a 'scolding wife'.
>
> (Archer, 1994c: 314)

It is tempting to imagine that, in the twenty-first century, such views are all but extinct. But that would be a mistake. Nancy Lombard's (2008) study reported Glaswegian children of primary-school age saying that if a woman did something wrong (such as cheat on her husband or boyfriend), then it wouldn't be unreasonable of him to respond in a violent manner. Hilde Jacobsen (2014) writes about how in Tanzania, a country renowned for its low levels of violence, wife-beating is widely accepted. She explains that many Tanzanian women work long hours (up to 16 hours a day) on farms owned by their husbands, i.e. in almost every sense, her husband is her boss; his authority is as good as absolute. In the minds of both partners, she is there to serve him; and if she fails to fulfil her duties or refuses to act upon his command, then she renders herself open to punishment. Indeed, Jacobsen notes that several of her Tanzanian respondents invoked the concept of a 'good beating' – a level of physical retribution proportionate to the original 'offence'.

A structural understanding of female abuse, then, sees violence as a sign of *trouble* within a (patriarchal) system. In theory at least, such societies will run quite harmoniously so long as everyone keeps to their designated roles, but as soon as somebody steps out of line, then trouble will erupt. In this sense, violence is both a sign of a system in crisis and also the means by which it attempts to repair itself, to get back to a state of running order. A 'good' beating restores the status quo. However, patriarchal societies are not held together by violence (and the threat of violence) alone. They rely, for the most part, upon the consent or support of the citizenry. Patriarchies, meaning, literally, the 'rule of the father', are serviced by a set of ideas (or ideologies) which hold that men have a natural or God-given authority over women. There was very clear evidence of such thinking amongst Jacobsen's respondents. Most of the men she spoke to saw themselves as heads of their respective households. As one put it, 'All final decisions are mine. Mine, because I am the [man]'. Crucially, though, many of the womenfolk subscribed to those same ideologies, which, in turn, coloured the way that they understood the violence perpetrated against them. Jacobsen offers the following quote from one young woman:

> A woman beaten a lot is a woman who wants to call the shots. She wants to be the man. She doesn't want to obey the man, she wants to be the man. She's the mother and she wants to be the father. That's where the problem starts.
>
> (Jacobsen, 2014: 550)

There are a number of things that stand out about such a statement. First and foremost is the way that these women place the blame for men's violence upon their own shoulders. It's *their* fault that they get a good beating, rather than their husbands'. A second is the way that the rule of the father is held to be at the very heart of what is to be a man. Akin to Butler's (1990) line of argument, it's as though gender *is* the performance; whoever 'calls the shots' is the man.

We can see traces of the same logic in studies based in other parts of the world. For example, Cristina Alcalde looked at the issue of domestic violence amongst Latin American men living and working in the US state of Kentucky (Alcalde, 2011). Most of the men she spoke to were Mexican immigrants who had crossed the border to take advantage of the work opportunities afforded by the US. However, some of the men felt that the move had put a strain on their relationships with their wives and girlfriends. Part of the problem, they said, was that, in the US, the law didn't permit men to conduct those relationships as they would back in Mexico. In the US, a man couldn't raise his hand to his partner, for fear of her going to the police. But they complained of other things, too. They thought that, culturally speaking, the US had a bad influence on their partners; they felt that they were being led astray by their American counterparts, free to do as they pleased, just 'like any man'. As 'Miguel' explained, 'Hispanic women think the man is the boss, American women don't think that way' (Alcalde, 2011: 461).

As we saw in Chapter 4, work has been, and remains, a crucial signifier of masculinity. In particular, being the breadwinner affords men a ready sense of dignity and purpose. We saw in Chapter 5 how difficult it can be for men to relinquish that role, or to find themselves on the other side of provider–dependent relationship. Sarah Hautzinger's (2003) study of gender relations in Brazil looks at just this situation. She describes how, within this particular economy, it is often easier for women to find paid employment. As a consequence, many also find themselves, for a while at least, in the position of being the major earner. This has led to frictions in many relationships, including domestic abuse. Hautzinger acknowledges that one of the most likely reasons for the outbreak of violence was men's attempt to compensate for their loss of face or status. Like others working in the same field, Hautzinger is of the opinion that where men lack more legitimate means of proving their masculinity, they will often resort to violence (Dobash and Dobash, 1992; Kaukinen, 2004; Totten, 2003). However, she also echoes Alcalde's analysis in seeing it as a distress signal born of the destabilisation of a broader system of gender relations in which men (and women) used to know their place.

SEXUAL VIOLENCE

Assessing the full extent of male violence is a fraught business. Crime statistics give us some indication, but these will only represent the tip of the iceberg. A much more realistic guide can be gleaned from social research which surveys people's experiences of different forms of violence. The findings from such studies make for sobering reading. For example, whilst the levels reported vary significantly from one country to the next, it appears to be the case that in some parts of the world, the *majority* of women experience abuse at the hands of men (World Health Organisation, 2005), the situation in sub-Saharan Africa being particularly serious (Jewkes, 2012). In the US, around 1 in 4 women say that they have been abused by men at some point in their lives. Unlike male-on-male violence, men's abuse of women is more typically located in the context of close or intimate relationships (past or present). One might have imagined that such environments offer a safe place for women – and, of course, they often do. But the plain fact is that if a woman is murdered, the most likely perpetrator is her husband or partner (Archer, 1994b).

In many respects, the picture regarding sexual violence is 'in tune' with that of domestic abuse more generally. In the West, we continue to peddle the myth of the rapist as a stranger lurking in the shadows, yet the research has shown, over and again, that sex offenders are much more likely to be someone well known to the victim – such as a boyfriend, work colleague or even a member of one's own family (Muehlenhard and Kimes, 1999). What is more, the abuse tends to be sustained, even chronic, rather than an isolated event (Frieze, 2005). Sexual offences cover an array of different activities: rape and sexual assault being the most obvious, but they also include things such as indecent exposure (or 'flashing'), human trafficking for sexual exploitation and the creation and/or selling of child pornography. In each of these respects, men make up the overwhelming majority of perpetrators; sexual abuse is the most gendered of all forms of violence. In terms of the prevalence of these crimes, again the figures vary (indeed, significantly so), but even at the lower reported levels the numbers are disconcerting. Surveys conducted in the US, UK and New Zealand all suggest that between 1 in 5 and 1 in 7 women have experienced rape (Pollard, 1994). The situation in other parts of the world is even bleaker. In their study of sexual violence in a South African township, Wood and Jewkes (2001) estimate that 30 per cent of girls lose their virginity through an act of enforced intercourse.

Given such findings, it is hardly surprising that feminists have been at the forefront of efforts both to theorise and combat sexual violence. Amongst their number, several have argued that such practices are a mainstay of patriarchy: a central mechanism by which men maintain their ascendant position in society (for example, MacKinnon, 1982; Scully, 1990; Wise and Stanley, 1987). Nowhere have these ideas been more clearly expressed than in a (now famous) declaration made by the American radical feminist Susan Brownmiller. She said:

> From prehistoric times to the present . . . rape has played a critical function. It is nothing more or less than a conscious process of intimidation by which all men keep all women in a state of fear.
> (Brownmiller, 1976: 15)

Inevitably, Brownmiller's statement caused quite a stir; some thought it simply outrageous, but the uncomfortable truth is that the reality lies closer to her assessment than many would care to imagine. Psychological studies of convicted rapists have shown that they are indistinguishable from the wider population of men in terms of their personality profiles (Pollard, 1994). In other words, rapists aren't a particular *type* of man. In his studies of the 'proclivity' (i.e. tendency or inclination) to rape, Neil Malamuth (1981) found that amongst a sample of 42 male college students, no less than 35 per cent said that, if they knew they could get away with it, they would be prepared to rape a women. Jewkes (2012) has suggested that around one third of South African men actually have committed the crime – and that the same could be said of about a quarter of Indian men. Furthermore, research conducted in the US has revealed that almost 1 in 4 male college students will admit to having coerced or put pressure on a girl to have sex (Kelly, 1988). Given such statistics, we can surely begin to understand why some have argued that rather than there being a clear-cut division between sexual predators and 'normal' men, there is more of a sliding scale or continuum. Not all men rape (of course), but some do, and a greater number still commit other, more minor, offences, such as coercion and sexual harassment.

A vivid picture of the 'everyday' nature of sexual harassment can be found in a study by Heather Hlavka (2014). Set in the US, her focus was on the experiences and understandings of girls aged between 11 and 16, in a culture where 'objectification, sexual harassment and abuse appear[ed] to be part of the fabric of young women's lives' (344). They were subject to abuse almost everywhere they went: at school, in the playground and at parties. The girls complained to Hlavka about the way that boys would follow them around, trying to touch or grope them, but at the same time, she noted, they would often dismiss such actions as 'no big deal'. 'It's okay', said one 13-year-old girl, 'because they do it to everyone'. The ubiquity of the harassment made it appear to them as normal – even natural. Indeed, the girls interpreted their interactions with boys through two of the more dominant *sexual stories* outlined in the previous chapter – where boys/men are construed as active, desirous and thrusting, whilst girls/women are viewed as passive, vulnerable and submissive. Within such a framing, the abusive nature of the boys' behaviour takes on the air of something inevitable. As another girl commented, 'They're boys – that's what they do'. Moreover, Hlavka explains that the girls didn't see the boys' actions as abusive because, in their estimations, abuse meant *rape* – which, in turn, was understood (narrowly) as enforced coitus. Hence, when one 11-year-old girl was pressurized into performing fellatio on a 17-year-old boy, she didn't understand this as rape (even though it fits the legal definition in the US and elsewhere). Indeed, she said that the boy had threatened to 'rape' her if she didn't do as she was told. It is little wonder that so much sexual violence goes unreported and unrecorded.

There are so many other aspects of sexual violence to which we might turn our attention were there no constraints on space. For example, we haven't looked at the patterns of abuse found in the relationships between gay men (Waldner-Haugrud *et al.*, 1997); neither have we explored those (significantly fewer) cases where men have been abused at the hands of women (Weiss, 2010). I haven't ventured into the literature on the sexual abuse of children (Browne, 1994) and nor have I found an opportunity to open up the highly complex debates around the role of pornography – particularly since the expansion of the internet (Antevska and Gavey, 2015). However, we do need to ask, finally, why are men so heavily implicated in these acts of sexual violence? Why those particular 'never-ending games of fear, pain and death'? As I hope I've shown throughout this book, the answer is not 'they're men: it's what they do'. Masculinity is not an essence; it doesn't make men rape and kill. Yet, in a strictly grammatical sense, it seems to me that Hlavka's young respondent was pretty close to the mark – or, at least, to a much more convincing line of explanation. Along with Judith Butler (1990), and an increasing number of other gender theorists, I would argue that masculinity *is* what men do. But they don't rape and kill – as well as work and love – *because* they are men; the logic runs in the opposite direction. They do these things in order to count as men, both in their own eyes and in the eyes of others.

NOTE

1 In July 2016, the UK government lifted its ban on women serving in the country's infantry, cavalry and armoured corps.

FURTHER READING

Canetto, S.S. (2015) 'Suicide: Why are older men so vulnerable?' *Men and Masculinities* (available online first).

This is a forensic analysis of why, in the US, older men of European descent are over-represented as suicide victims. In examining various hypotheses, Canetto touches upon broader debates about the relationship between suicide and masculinity.

Gender and Society (2016), 30(1).

This is a special issue of the journal dedicated to the subject of rape. It is comprised of nine articles covering a range of contexts including war and college campuses. This is research at the cutting edge.

Goldstein, A.P. (1994) 'Delinquent Gangs'. In J. Archer (ed.) *Male Violence*. London: Routledge (87–104).

This chapter reflects upon the way that gang life has been understood in recent years – from a bunch of degenerates to a surrogate family. Goldstein looks at the composition of US gangs and considers various attempts, on the part of the authorities, to deal with gang-related violence.

Gossett, J.L. and Byrne, S. (2002) '"Click Here": A content analysis of internet rape sites'. *Gender and Society*, 16(5): 689–709.
A rather disturbing glimpse into the world of violent pornography on the internet. As part of their analysis, they discuss the 'racialisation' of the victims on these sites.

Lips, H.M. (2014) 'Global Patterns of Gender-related Violence. In *Gender: The Basics*. London: Routledge (118–141).
Lips provides a (necessarily) short but wide-ranging review of gender-related violence, including sections on violence between gay couples, violent pornography and the problems of sex trafficking.

GLOSSARY

Age of Reason: the period, beginning in eighteenth-century Europe, when the authority of religious doctrine was overtaken by science and rationality.

Agrarian society: one based upon farming or the cultivation of the land.

Androcentrism: a view of the world that sees masculinity or maleness as standard.

Anorexia: a very serious eating disorder involving drastic restrictions in food intake.

Bulimia: another serious eating disorder which involves an alternation of binging on and purging of food.

Consumerism: a cultural emphasis on the acquisition of goods and services (where shopping is seen as a pastime).

Dimorphic brain: the assumption that there are two forms of the human brain: one male, the other female.

Ethnographic: a style of research that aims to provide a close description of ordinary people's lives from their point of view.

Feminism: first and second waves: two phases of the women's movement. The first wave (around the turn of the twentieth century) was focused upon the campaign to gain the vote; the second (during the 1960s and 70s) pursued issues such as reproductive rights and equal-pay legislation.

Globalisation: a process of increased international inter-dependency involving the movement of goods, ideas and people.

Heteronormative: a view of the world that treats the coupling of men and women as standard.

Homophobia: literally, *fear* of homosexuality. More generally, the despising and disapproval of gay people and gay lifestyles.

Human Genome Project: a project launched in 1990 with the aim of mapping the chemical sequence of every gene in a single human body.

Hysteria: a rather old-fashioned term to describe a nervous or emotional disorder which manifests in physical symptoms.

Mesomorphic: an athletic body shape comprising broad shoulders tapering to a slim waist.

Metrosexual: a mode of masculinity in which appearance and style has great emphasis. The metrosexual man is impeccably groomed.

Movember: a now global campaign to raise awareness about men's health issues, support for which is signified by the growing of moustaches across the month of November.

Neo-liberalism: the doctrine of economic liberalisation and a feature of the global economy since the early 1980s.

Pan sexuality: an erotic attraction to the full array of gender and sexual identities: men, women and trans, gay, straight and bisexual.

Patriarchy: literally, the rule of the father. A social and cultural system that systematically privileges men and masculinity.

Polysexuality: an erotic attraction to many (but not all) gender and sexual identities (see **pan sexuality**).

Retributive man: a traditional form of masculinity: dominant, competitive, stoical and not at all interested in fashion and grooming products!

Role theory: a sociological theory that assumes much of human behaviour is the playing out of predetermined scripts.

Social learning theory: the theory that people learn all that it is to be human through encouragement, punishment and copying.

Testosterone: the male sex hormone produced by the testes and responsible for the development of secondary sexual characteristics in men.

BIBLIOGRAPHY

Acker, J. (1990) 'Hierarchies, Jobs, Bodies: A theory of gendered organization'. *Gender and Society*, 4: 139–58.

Adams, M.L. (2005) '"Death to the Prancing Prince": Effeminacy, sport discourses and the salvation of men's dancing'. *Body & Society*, 11(4): 63–86.

Ahmad, Y. and Smith, P.K. (1994) *Bullying in Schools and the Issue of Sex Differences*. In J. Archer (ed.) *Male Violence*. London: Routledge (70–83).

Alcalde, M.C. (2011) 'Masculinities in Motion: Latino men and violence in Kentucky'. *Men and Masculinities*, 14(4): 450–69.

Allen, L. (2003) 'Girls Want Sex, Boys Want Love: Resisting dominant discourses of (hetero)sexuality'. *Sexualities*, 6(2): 215–36.

Allen, S. and Daly, K.J. (2007) *The Effects of Father Involvement: A Summary of the Research Evidence* (2nd. edition). Guelph, ON: Health Canada.

Altman, D. (1972) *Homosexual: Oppression and Liberation*. Sydney: Angus and Robertson.

Altman, M. (1984) 'Everything They Always Wanted to Know: The ideology of popular sex literature'. In C. Vance (ed.) *Pleasure and Danger*. Boston: Routledge & Kegan Paul (115–30).

Amato, P.R and Sobolewski, J.M. (2004) 'The Effects of Divorce on Fathers and Children'. In M.E. Lamb (ed.) *The Role of the Father in Child Development* (4th. edition). Hoboken, NJ: Wiley & Sons.

Anderson, E. (2009) *Inclusive Masculinity: The Changing Nature of Masculinities*. London: Routledge.

Anderson, E. and McCormack, M. (2015) 'Cuddling and Spooning: Heteromasculinity and homosocial tactility among student-athletes'. *Men and Masculinities*, 18(2): 214–30.

Anderson, K.L. and Umberson, D. (2001) 'Gendering Violence: Masculinity and power in men's accounts of domestic violence'. *Gender and Society*, 15(3): 358–80.

Antevska, A. and Gavey, N. (2015) '"Out of Sight and Out of Mind": Detachment and men's consumption of male sexual dominance and female submission in pornography'. *Men and Masculinities*, 18(5): 605–29.

Archer, D., Iritani, B., Kimes, D.B. and Barrios, M. (1983) 'Face-ism: Five studies of sex differences in facial prominence'. *Journal of Personality and Social Psychology*, 45(4): 725–35.

Archer, J. (ed.) (1994a) *Male Violence*. London: Routledge.

Archer, J. (1994b) 'Violence between Men'. In J. Archer (ed.) *Male Violence*. London: Routledge (121–40).

Archer, J. (1994c) 'Power and Male Violence'. In J. Archer (ed.) *Male Violence*. London: Routledge. (310–31).

Arnold, J.H. and Brady, S. (eds) (2011) *What is Masculinity? Historical Dynamics from Antiquity to the Contemporary World*. New York: Palgrave Macmillan.

Ashbourne, L.M., Daly, K.J. and Brown, J.L. (2011) 'Responsiveness in Father-Child Relationships: The experience of fathers'. *Fathering*, 9(1): 69–86.

Astone, N.M. and Peters, H.E. (2014) 'Longitudinal Influences on Men's Lives: Research from the transition to fatherhood project and beyond'. *Fathering*, 12(2): 161–73.

Atkins, D. (1998) *Looking Queer: Body Image and Identity in Lesbian, Bisexual, Gay and Transgendered Communities*. New York: Harrington Park Press.

Atkinson, M. (2011) *Deconstructing Men and Masculinities*. Oxford: Oxford University Press.

Attwood, F. (2006) 'Sexed Up: Theorizing the sexualization of culture'. *Sexualities*, 9(1): 77–94.

Bandura, A. (1977) *Social Learning Theory*. Englewood Cliffs, NJ: Prentice-Hall.

Barrett, F.J. (2001) 'The Organizational Construction of Hegemonic Masculinity: The case of the US Navy'. In S.M. Whitehead and F.J. Barrett (eds) *The Masculinities Reader*. Cambridge: Polity (77–99).

Bartky, S. (1990) *Femininity and Domination: Studies in the Phenomenology of Oppression*. New York: Routledge.

Beauvoir, S. de [1949] (1953) *The Second Sex*. London: Cape.

Bech, H. (2003) 'The Disappearance of the Modern Homosexual'. In J. Weeks, J. Holland and M. Waites (eds) *Sexualities and Society: A Reader*. Cambridge: Polity (277–87).

Bem, S.L. (1974) 'The Measurement of Psychological Androgyny'. *Journal of Consulting and Clinical Psychology*, 42: 155–62.

Benatar, D. (2012) *The Second Sexism: Discrimination against Men and Boys*. Oxford: Wiley-Blackwell.

Benedict, J. and Klein, A. (1997) 'Arrest and Conviction Rates for Athletes Accused of Sexual Assault'. *Sociology of Sport Journal*, 14: 86–94.

Billig, M., Condor, S., Edwards, D., Gane, M., Middleton, D. and Radley, A. (1988) *Ideological Dilemmas: A Social Psychology of Everyday Thinking*. London: Sage.

Bittman, M. (2004) 'Parenting and Employment: What time-use surveys show'. In N. Folbre and M. Bittman (eds) *Family Time: The Social Organization of Care*. London: Routledge (152–70).

Bly, J. (1990) *Iron John*. New York: Addison-Wesley.

Bowlby, J. (1951) *Maternal Care and Mental Health*. Geneva: World Health Organisation.

Bordo, S. (1999) *The Male Body: A New Look at Men in Public and Private*. New York: Farrar, Straus and Giroux.

Brannon, R. (1976) 'The Male Sex Role: Our culture's blueprint of manhood, and what it's done for us lately'. In D. David and R. Brannon (eds) *The Forty-Nine Percent Majority: The Male Sex Role*. Reading, MA: Addison-Wesley (1–45).

Braun, V., Gavey, N. and McPhillips, K. (2003) 'The "Fair Deal"? Unpacking accounts of reciprocity in heterosex'. *Sexualities*, 6(2): 237–61.

Bridges, T.S. (2009) 'Gender Capital and Male Bodybuilders'. *Body & Society*, 15(1): 83–107.

Brittan, A. (1989) *Masculinity and Power*. New York: Blackwell.

Browne, K. (1994) 'Child Sexual Abuse'. In J. Archer (ed.) *Male Violence*. London: Routledge (210–30).

Brownmiller, S. (1976) *Against Our Will: Men, Women and Rape*. Harmondsworth: Penguin.

Buller, D.J. (2005) *Adapting Minds: Evolutionary Psychology and the Persistent Quest for Human Nature*. Cambridge, MA: MIT Press.

Butler, J. (1990) *Gender Trouble: Feminism and the Subversion of Identity*. New York: Routledge.

Butler, J. (1992) 'The Body You Want: Liz Kotz interviews Judith Butler'. *Artforum*, 31(3) (November): 82–9.

Bzostek, S.H. (2008) 'Social Fathers and Child Well-Being'. *Journal of Marriage and Family*, 70(4): 950–61.

Calasanti, T. and King, N. (2005) 'Firming the Floppy Penis: Age, class and gender relations in the lives of old men'. *Men and Masculinities*, 8(1): 3–23.

Campbell, A. and Muncer, S. (1994) 'Men and the Meaning of Violence'. In J. Archer (ed.) *Male Violence*. London: Routledge (332–51).

Canetto, S.S. (2015) 'Suicide: Why are older men so vulnerable?' *Men and Masculinities* (available online first). Retrieved 20 May 2016 from: http://journals.sagepub.com/doi/full/10.1177/1097184X15613832.

Carpenter, L.M. (2002) 'Gender and the Meaning and Experience of Virginity Loss in the Contemporary United States'. *Gender and Society*, 16(3): 345–65.

Carrigan, T., Connell, R.W. and Lee, J. (1985) 'Towards a New Sociology of Masculinity'. *Theory and Society*, 14(5): 551–604.

Carson, J.L, and Parke, R.D. (1996) 'Reciprocal Negative Affect in Parent-Child Interactions and Children's Peer Competency'. *Child Development*, 67: 2217–26.

Chambers, D. (2001) *Representing the Family*. London: Sage.

Chapman, R. and Rutherford, J. (eds) (1988) *Male Order: Unwrapping Masculinity*. London: Lawrence & Wishart.

Chesler, P. (1978) *About Men*. New York: Simon & Schuster.

Chesley, N. (2011) 'Stay-at-home Fathers and Breadwinning Mothers: Gender, couple dynamics, and social change'. *Gender and Society*, 25, 642–64.

Chodorow, N. (1978) *The Reproduction of Mothering: Psychoanalysis and the Sociology of Gender*. Berkeley, CA: University of California Press.

Chodorow, N. (1989) *Feminism and Psychoanalytic Theory*. New Haven, CT: Yale University Press.

Clare, A. (2000) *On Men: Masculinity in Crisis*. London: Chatto and Windus.

Cockburn, C. (1985) *Machinery of Dominance: Women, Men and Technical Know-How*. London: Pluto Press.

Cohane, G.H. and Pope, H.G. (2001) 'Body Image in Boys: A review of the literature'. *International Journal of Eating Disorders*, 29: 373–79.

Cohen, B. (1988) *Caring for Children. Services and Policies for Childcare and Equal Opportunities in the United Kingdom*. London: Family Policy Studies Centre.

Cohen, D. (1990) *Being a Man*. London: Routledge.

Collinson, D.L. and Hearn, J. (eds) (1996) *Men as Managers, Managers as Men: Critical Perspectives on Men, Masculinities and Management*. London: Sage.

Connell, R.W. (1987) *Gender and Power*. Cambridge: Polity Press.

Connell, R.W. (1995) *Masculinities*. Cambridge: Polity.

Connell, R.W. (2000) 'Arms and the Man: Using the new research on masculinity to understand violence and promote peace in the contemporary world'. In I. Breines, R.W. Connell and I. Eide (eds) *Male Roles, Masculinities and Violence: A Culture of Peace Perspective*. Paris: UNESCO Publishing (21–33).

Connell, R.W. (2009) *Gender: In World Perspective* (2nd. edition). Cambridge: Polity.

Connell, R.W. and Wood, J. (2005) 'Globalization and Business Masculinities'. *Men and Masculinities*, 7(4): 347–64.

Craig, L. (2006) 'Parental Education, Time in Paid Work and Time with Children: An Australian time-diary analysis'. *British Journal of Sociology*, 57(4): 553–75.

Culp, R.E., Crook, A.S. and Housley, P.C. (1983) 'A Comparison of Observed and Reported Adult-Infant Interactions: Effects of perceived sex'. *Sex Roles*, 9: 475–9.

Curry, T.J. (1993) 'A Little Pain Never Hurt Anyone: Athletic career socialisation and the normalisation of sports injury'. *Symbolic Interaction*, 16(3): 273–90.

Curry, T.J. (2000) 'Booze and Bar Fights: A journey to the dark side of college athletics'. In J. McKay, M.A. Messner and D. Sabo (eds) *Masculinities, Gender Relations and Sport*. Thousand Oaks, CA: Sage (162–75).

Daly, K. (1993) 'Reshaping Fatherhood: Finding the models'. *Journal of Family Issues*, 14(4): 510–30.

Daly, M. and Wilson, M. (1994) 'Evolutionary Psychology of Male Violence'. In J. Archer (ed.) *Male Violence*. London: Routledge (253–88).

Darwin, C. (1871) *The Descent of Man, and Selection in Relation to Sex*. London: John Murray.

Davis, K. (2002) 'A Dubious Equality: Men, women and cosmetic surgery'. *Body and Society*, 8(1): 49–65.

Davis, K. (ed.) (1997) *Embodied Practices*. London: Sage.

Dawson, G. (1994) *Soldier Heroes: British Adventure, Empire and the Imagining of Masculinities*. London: Routledge.

Delamont, S. (1995) 'Sex Stereotyping in the Classroom'. In B. Moon and A. Shelton Mayes (eds) *Teaching and Learning in the Secondary School*. Buckingham: Open University Press (187–91).

Delphy, C. (1984) *Close to Home: A Materialist Analysis of Woman's Oppression*. London: Hutchinson.

Dennis, N. and Erdos, G. (2000) *Families without Fatherhood* (3rd. edition). London: Institute for the Study of Civil Society.

Department of Education (2011) *Research Report DFE-RR151*. Retrieved 18 December 2015 from: https://www.gov.uk/government/uploads/system/uploads/attachment_data/file/182407/DFE-RR151.pdf.

Dermott, E. (2008) *Intimate Fatherhood: A Sociological Analysis*. London: Routledge.

Dobash, R. and Dobash, R.E. (1992) *Women, Violence and Social Change*. New York: Routledge.

Doucet, A. (2006) *Do Men Mother? Fathering, Care and Domestic Responsibility*. Toronto: University of Toronto Press.

Dowsett, G.W. (1996) *Practicing Desire: Homosexual Sex in the Era of AIDS*. Stanford, CA: University of Stanford Press.

Duncombe, J. and Marsden, D. (1996) 'Whose Orgasm Is This Anyway? "Sex work" in long-term heterosexual couple relationships'. In J. Weeks and J. Holland (eds) *Sexual Cultures: Communities, Values and Intimacy*. London: Macmillan (220–38).

Dunning, E. (1986) 'Sport as Male Preserve'. *Theory, Culture and Society*, 3(1): 79–90.

Dunning, E. (1999) *Sport Matters: Sociological Studies of Sport, Violence and Civilisation*. London: Routledge.

Dyer, R. (1993) *The Matter of Images: Essays on Representations*. London: Routledge.

Dyer, R. (2002) 'The White Man's Muscles'. In R. Adams and D. Savran (eds) *The Masculinity Reader*. Oxford: Blackwell (262–73).

Eck, B.A. (2014) 'Compromising Positions: Unmarried men, heterosexuality and two-phase masculinity'. *Men and Masculinities*, 17(2): 147–72.

Edley, N. and Wetherell, M. (1995) *Men in Perspective: Practice, Power and Identity*. Hemel Hempstead: Prentice Hall/Harvester Wheatsheaf.

Edley, N. and Wetherell, M. (1997) 'Jockeying for Position: The construction of masculine identities' *Discourse and Society*, 8(2): 203–17.

Edley, N. and Wetherell, M. (1999) 'Imagined Futures: Young men's talk about fatherhood and domestic life'. *British Journal of Social Psychology*, 38(2): 181–94.

Edley, N. (2006) 'Never the Twain Shall Meet: A critical appraisal of the combination of discourse and psychoanalytic theory in studies of men and masculinity'. *Sex Roles*, 55(9/10): 601–8.

Edwards, T. (1997) *Men in the Mirror: Men's Fashion, Masculinity and Consumer Society*. London: Cassell.

Eggebeen, D.J., Knoester, C. and McDaniel, B. (2013) 'The Implications of Fatherhood for Men'. In N. Cabrera and C.S. Tamis-LeMonda (eds) *Handbook of Father Involvement: Multidisciplinary Perspectives* (2nd. edition). New York: Routledge (338–57).

Ehrenreich, B. (1987) *Remaking Love*. London: Fontana Collins.

Einstein, G. (ed.) (2007) *Sex and the Brain*. Cambridge, MA: MIT Press.

Enloe, C. (2004) 'Wielding Masculinity inside Abu Ghraib: Making feminist sense of an American military scandal'. *Asian Journal of Women's Studies*, 10(3): 89–102.

Falk, P. (1994) *The Consuming Body*. London: Sage.

Falk, P. (1995) 'Written in the Flesh'. *Body & Society*, 1(1): 95–105.

Faludi, S. (1992) *Backlash: The Undeclared War against Women*. London: Chatto and Windus.

Farr, R.H., Forssell, S.L. and Patterson, C.J. (2010) 'Parenting and Child Development in Adoptive Families: Does parental sexual orientation matter?' *Applied Developmental Science*, 14(3): 164–78.

Farrell, W. (1974) *The Liberated Man*. New York: Random House.

Farrell, W. (1994) *The Myth of Male Power*. New York: Fourth Estate.

Farrell, W. and Sterba, J.P. (2008) *Does Feminism Discriminate against Men?* Oxford: Oxford University Press.

Fausto-Sterling, A. (2000) *Sexing the Body: Gender Politics and the Construction of Sexuality*. New York: Basic Books.

Fasteau, M.F. (1974) *The Male Machine*. New York: McGraw-Hill.

Featherstone, M. (1991) *Consumer Culture and Postmodernism*. London: Sage.

Figes, K. (2013) *Our Cheating Hearts: Love and Loyalty, Lust and Lies*. London: Virago.

Fine, C. (2010) *Delusions of Gender: How Our Minds, Society, and Neurosexism Create Difference*. London: Icon Books.

Fishman, P. (1978) 'Interaction: The work women do'. *Social Problems*, 25, 397–406.

Forste, R., Bartkowski, J.P. and Jackson, R.A. (2009) '"Just Be There For Them": Perceptions of fathering among single, low-income men'. *Fathering*, 7(1): 49–69.

Foucault, M. (1979) *The History of Sexuality. Vol. 1. An Introduction*. London: Allen Lane.

Franklin, C.W. (1993) 'Ain't I a Man? The efficacy of black masculinities for men's studies in the 1990s'. In R. Major and J.V. Gordon (eds) *The American Black Male: His Present Status and His Future*. Chicago, IL: Nelson Hall (285–99).

Freud, S. (1912) 'On the Universal Tendency to Debasement in the Sphere of Love'. *Standard Edition 11*: 177–96.

Frieze, I.H. (2005) *Hurting the One You Love: Violence in Intimate Relationships*. Belmont, CA: Wadworth/Thompson Learning.

Frosh, S. (1987) *The Politics of Psychoanalysis: An Introduction to Freudian and Post-Freudian Theory*. London: Macmillan.

Frosh, S., Phoenix, A. and Pattman, R. (2002) *Young Masculinities: Understanding Boys in Contemporary Society*. Basingstoke: Palgrave.

Froyum, C.M. (2007) '"At Least I'm Not Gay": Heterosexual identity making among poor black teens'. *Sexualities*, 10(5): 603–22.

Gagnon, J.H. and Simon, W. (1973) *Sexual Conduct: The Social Sources of Human Sexuality*. London: Hutchinson.

Gaines, S. and Churcher, S. (1994) *Obsession: The Lives and Times of Calvin Klein*. New York: Avon Books.

Garfinkel, H. (1967) *Studies in Ethnomethodology*. Englewood Cliffs, NJ: Prentice Hall.

Gattrell, C. (2007) 'Whose Child is it Anyway? The negotiation of paternal entitlements within marriage'. *The Sociological Review*, 55(2): 352–72.

Gavey, N., McPhillips, K. and Braun, V. (1999) '*Interruptus Coitus*: Heterosexuals accounting for intercourse'. *Sexualities*, 2(1): 35–68.

Gerschick, T.J and Miller, A.S. (1995) 'Coming to Terms: Masculinity and physical disability'. In D.F. Sabo and D.F. Gordon (eds) *Men's Health and Illness: Gender, Power and the Body. Research on Men and Masculinities Series, Vol. 8*. Thousand Oaks, CA: Sage (183–204).

Giddens, A. (1991) *Modernity and Self-identity: Self and Society in Late Modern Age*. London: Polity Press.

Gilbert, P. (1994) 'Male Violence: Towards an integration'. In J. Archer (ed.) *Male Violence*. London: Routledge (352–89).

Gill, R. (2007) *Gender and the Media*. Cambridge: Polity.

Gill, R., Henwood, K. and McLean, C. (2005) 'Body Projects and the Regulation of Normative Masculinity'. *Body and Society*. 11(1): 37–62.

Gilligan, J. (2010) 'Culture, Gender and Violence: "We are not women"'. In M.S. Kimmel and M.A. Messner (eds) *Men's Lives* (8th. edition). Boston: Allyn & Bacon (551–8).

Gillis, J. (1995) 'Bringing up Father: British paternal identities, 1700 to the present'. *Masculinities*, 3(3): 1–27.

Gilmartin, S.K. (2007) 'Crafting Heterosexual Masculine Identities on Campus'. *Men and Masculinities*, 9(4): 530–9.

Goffman, E. (1979) *Gender Advertisements*. London: Macmillan.

Goldberg, A.E. (2009) *Lesbian and Gay Parents and Their Children: Research on the Family Life Cycle*. Washington, DC: American Psychological Society.

Goldberg, H. (1976) *The Hazards of Being Male: Surviving the Myth of Male Privilege*. New York: Nash.

Goldhill, S. (2004) *Love, Sex and Tragedy: How the Ancient World Shapes Our Lives*. University of Chicago: University of Chicago Press.

Goldstein, A.P. (1994) 'Delinquent Gangs'. In J. Archer (ed.) *Male Violence*. London: Routledge (87–104).

Goode-Cross, D.T. and Good, G.E. (2008) 'African American Men Who Have Sex With Men: Creating safe spaces through relationships'. *Psychology of Men & Masculinity*, 9(4): 221–34.

Goodwin, N.R., Ackerman, F. and Kiron, D. (eds) (1997) *The Consumer Society*. Washington, DC: Island Press.

Gossett, J.L. and Byrne, S. (2002) '"Click Here": A content analysis of internet rape sites'. *Gender and Society*, 16(5): 689–709.

Gramsci, A. (1971) *Selections from Prison Notebooks*. London: Lawrence and Wishart.

Gray, J. (1995) *Mars and Venus in the Bedroom: A Lasting Guide to Romance and Passion*. New York: Harper Collins.

Greenson, R. (1968) 'Dis-identifying from Mother: Its special importance for the boy'. *International Psychoanalytic Journal*, 49: 370–4.

Grbich, C. (1995) 'Male Primary Caregivers and Domestic Labour: Involvement or avoidance?'. *Journal of Family Studies*, 1(2): 114–29.

Grogan, S. and Richards, H. (2002) 'Body Image: Focus groups with boys and men'. *Men and Masculinities*, 4(3): 219–32.

Grosz, E. (1994) *Volatile Bodies: Toward a Corporeal Feminism*. Bloomington, IN: Indiana University Press.

Guasch, O. (2011) 'Social Stereotypes and Masculine Homosexualities: The Spanish case'. *Sexualities*, 14(5): 526–43.

Gunter, B. (1986) *Television and Sex Role Stereotyping*. London: John Libby.

Hacker, S. (1989) *Power, Pleasure and Technology*. Boston: Unwin Hyman.

Halberstam, J. (1998) *Female Masculinity*. London: Duke University Press.

Hall, C. (1992) *White, Male and Middle Class: Explorations in Feminism and History*. Cambridge: Polity Press.

Hannon, V. (1981) *Ending Sex-Stereotyping in Schools: A Sourcebook for School-based Teacher Workshops*. Manchester: Equal Opportunities Commission.

Harrison, J. (1978) 'Warning: the male sex role may be dangerous to your health'. *Journal of Social Issues*, 34(1): 65–86.

Harstock, N. (1989) 'Masculinity, Heroism and the Making of War'. In A. Harris and Y. King (eds) *Rocking the Ship of State: Towards a Feminist Peace Politics*. Boulder, CO: Westview (133–52).

Hartmann, H. (1979) 'The Unhappy Marriage of Marxism and Feminism: Towards a more progressive union'. *Capital and Class*, 8: 1–33.

Harvey, D. (2005) *A Brief History of Neoliberalism*. Oxford: Oxford University Press.

Hautzinger, S. (2003) 'Researching Men's Violence'. *Men and Masculinities*, 6(1): 93–106.

Haywood, C. and Mac an Ghaill, M. (2003) *Men and Masculinities*. Buckingham: Open University Press.

Hearn, J. (1987) *The Gender of Oppression: Men, Masculinity and the Critique of Marxism*. Brighton: Harvester Wheatsheaf.

Heasley, R. (2005) 'Queer Masculinities of Straight Men'. *Men and Masculinities*, 7(3): 310–20.

Henley, N. (1977) *Body Politics: Power, Sex and Nonverbal Communication*. Englewood Cliffs, NJ: Prentice Hall.

Hewlett, B.S. (1991) *Intimate Fathers*. Ann Arbor, MI: University of Michigan Press.

Higate, P. and Hopton, J. (2005) 'War, Militarism and Masculinities'. In M.S. Kimmel, J. Hearn and R.W. Connell (eds) *Handbook of Studies on Men and Masculinities*. London: Sage (432–47).

Hill Collins, P. and Bilge, S. (2016) *Intersectionality*. Hoboken, NJ: Wiley & Sons.

Hise, R. (2004) *The War against Men*. Oakland, CA: Elderberry Press.

Hite, S. (1976) *The Hite Report on Female Sexuality*. New York: Macmillan.

Hite, S. (1990) *The Hite Report on Male Sexuality*. London: Optima.

Hlavka, H.R. (2014) 'Normalizing Sexual Violence: Young women account for harassment and abuse'. *Gender and Society*, 28(3): 337–58.

Hoch, P. (1979) *White Hero, Black Beast: Racism, Sexism and the Mask of Masculinity*. London: Pluto Press.

Hollander, J.A. (2001) 'Vulnerability and Dangerousness: The construction of gender through conversation about violence'. *Gender and Society*, 15(1): 83–109.

Hollway, W. (1984) 'Gender Difference and the Production of Subjectivity'. In J. Henriques, W. Hollway, C. Urwin, C. Venn and V. Walkerdine (eds) *Changing the Subject: Psychology, Social Regulation and Subjectivity*. London: Methuen (227–63).

Hollway, W. (1989) *Subjectivity and Method in Psychology*. London: Sage.

Holter, O.G. (2007) 'Men's Work and Family Reconciliation in Europe'. *Men and Masculinities*, 9(4): 425–65.

Horrocks, R. (1994) *Masculinity in Crisis: Myths, Fantasies and Realities*. Basingstoke: Palgrave.

Hudson, J.I., Hiripi, E., Pope, H.G. and Kessler, R.C. (2007) 'The Prevalence and Correlates of Eating Disorders in the National Comorbidity Survey Replication'. *Biological Psychiatry*, 61: 348–58.

Humphries, M. (1985) 'Gay Machismo'. In A. Metcalf and M. Humphries (eds) *The Sexuality of Men*. London: Pluto Press (70–85).

Hutchings, K. (2008) 'Making Sense of Masculinity and War'. *Men and Masculinities*, 10(4): 389–404.

Jackson, D. (1990) *Unmasking Masculinity: A Critical Autobiography*. London: Unwin Hyman.

Jacobsen, H. (2014) 'What's Gendered about Gender-based Violence? An empirically grounded theoretical exploration from Tanzania'. *Gender and Society*, 28(4): 537–61.

Janowitz, M. (1960) *The Professional Soldier*. New York: Free Press.

Jayakody, R. and Kahil, A. (2002) 'Social Fathering in Low-income, African American Families with Pre-school Children'. *Journal of Marriage and Family*, 64(2): 504–16.

Jewkes, R. (2012) *Rape Perpetration: A Review*. Pretoria: Sexual Violence Research Institute.

Johansson, T. (2011) 'Fatherhood in Transition: Paternity leave and changing masculinities'. *Journal of Family Communication*, 11(3): 165–80.

Johnson, M. (2010) '"Just Getting Off": The inseparability of ejaculation and hegemonic masculinity'. *Journal of Men's Studies*, 18(3): 238–48.

Jones, J. and Pugh, S. (2005) 'Ageing Gay Men: Lessons from the sociology of embodiment'. *Men and Masculinities*, 7(3): 248–60.

Jordan-Young, R.M. (2010) *Brain Storm: The Flaws in the Science of Sex Differences*. Cambridge, MA: Harvard University Press.

Kan, M.Y., Sullivan, O. and Gershuny, J. (2011) 'Gender Convergence in Domestic Work: Discerning the effects of interactional and institutional barriers from large-scale data'. *Sociology*, 45: 234–51.

Kanter, R.M (1977) *Men and Women of the Corporation*. New York: Basic Books.

Kaukinen, C. (2004) 'Status Compatibility, Physical Violence and Emotional Abuse in Intimate Relationships'. *Journal of Marriage and the Family*, 66(2): 452–71.

Kerfoot, D. and Knights, D. (1996) '"The Best is Yet to Come?": The quest for embodiment in managerial work'. In D.L. Collinson and J. Hearn (eds) *Men as Managers, Managers as Men: Critical Perspectives on Men, Masculinities and Management*. London: Sage (78–98).

Kelly, L. (1988) *Surviving Sexual Violence*. Cambridge: Polity.

Kiernan, K., McLanahan, S., Holmes, J. and Wright, M. (2011) 'Fragile Families in the US and UK'. *Center for Research on Child Well-Being, Princeton University, Working Paper WP*.

Kimmel, M.S. (ed.) (1987) *Changing Men: New Directions in the Study of Men and Masculinity*. Newbury Park, CA: Sage.

Kimmel, M.S. (1990) 'Baseball and the Reconstitution of American Masculinity, 1880–1920'. In M.A. Messner and D.F. Sabo (eds) *Sport, Men and the Gender Order: Critical Feminist Perspectives*. Champaign, IL: Human Kinetics (55–66).

Kimmel, M.S. (2001) 'Masculinity as Homophobia: Fear, shame and silence in the construction of gender identity'. In S. Whitehead and F. Barrett (eds) *The Masculinities Reader*. Cambridge: Polity (266–87).

Kimmel, M.S. (2012) *The History of Men: Essays on the History of American and British Masculinities*. Albany, NY: State University of New York Press.

Kimmel, M.S. and Messner, M.A. (2012) (eds) *Men's Lives* (9th. edition). Boston: Allyn & Bacon.

Kinsey, A.C., Pomeroy, W.B. and Martin, C.E. (1948) *Sexual Behaviour in the Human Male*. Philadelphia: W.B. Saunders.

Klein, J. (2006) 'Cultural Capital and High School Bullies'. *Men and Masculinities*, 9(1): 53–75.

Lamb, M.E. (ed.) (2004) *The Role of the Father in Child Development* (4th. edition). Hoboken, NJ: Wiley & Sons.

Lamb, M.E. (ed.) (2010) *The Role of the Father in Child Development* (5th. edition). Hoboken, NJ: Wiley & Sons.

Lamb, M.E. and Tamis-LeMonda, C.S. (2004) 'The Role of the Father: An introduction'. In M.E. Lamb (ed.) *The Role of the Father in Child Development*. (4th. edition). Hoboken, NJ: Wiley & Sons (1–31).

La Rossa, R. (1997) *The Modernization of Fatherhood: A Social and Political History*. London: University of Chicago Press.

Lehne, G. (1998) 'Homophobia among Men: Supporting and defining the male role'. In M. Kimmel and M. Messner (eds) *Men's Lives*, (4th. edition). Boston, MA: Allyn & Bacon (237–49).

Leidner, R. (1991) 'Serving Hamburgers and Selling Insurance: Gender, work, and identity in interactive service jobs'. *Gender and Society*, 5(2): 154–77.

Levant, R.F., Hirsch, L.S., Celentano, E., Cozza, T.M., Hill, S., MacEachern, M., Marty, N. and Schnedeker, J. (1992) 'The Male Role: An investigation of norms and stereotypes'. *Journal of Mental Health Counselling*, 14: 325–37.

Levesque, M.J. and Vichesky, D.R. (2006) 'Raising the Bar on the Body Beautiful: An analysis of the body image concerns of homosexual men'. *Body Image*, 3: 45–55.

Lindsey, E.W., Mize, J. and Pettit, G.S. (1997) 'Mutuality in Parent-Child Play: Consequences for children's peer competence'. *Journal of Social and Personal Relationships*, 14: 523–38.

Linton, R. (1936) *The Study of Man*. New York: Appleton-Century.

Lips, H. (1981) *Women, Men and the Psychology of Power*. Englewood Cliffs, NJ: Prentice Hall.

Lips, H.M. (2014) 'Global Patterns of Gender-related Violence'. In *Gender: The Basics*. London: Routledge (118–41).

Lombard, N. (2008) '"It's Wrong for a Boy to Hit a Girl because the Girl Might Cry": Investigating primary school children's attitudes towards violence against women'. In K. Throsby and F. Alexander (eds) *Gender and Interpersonal Violence: Language, Action and Representation*. Basingstoke: Palgrave (121–38).

Lorber, J. and Farrell, S.A. (eds) (1991) *The Social Construction of Gender*. London: Sage.

Lupton, D. and Barclay, L. (1997) *Constructing Fatherhood: Discourses and Experiences*. London: Sage.

Lyndon, N. (1992) *No More Sex War: The Failures of Feminism*. London: Sinclair Stevenson.

McArdle, K.A. and Hill, M.S. (2009) 'Understanding Body Dissatisfaction in Gay and Heterosexual Men'. *Men and Masculinities*, 11(5): 511–32.

McCarthy, B. (1994) 'Warrior Values: A socio-historical analysis'. In J. Archer (ed.) *Male Violence*. London: Routledge (105–20).

Maccoby, E. and Jacklin, C.N. (1974) *The Psychology of Sex Differences*. London: Oxford University Press.

McDowell, L. (2003) *Redundant Masculinities? Employment Change and White Working Class Youth*. Oxford: Blackwell.

Machin, A.J. (2015) 'Mind the Gap: The expectation and reality of involved fatherhood'. *Fathering*, 13(1): 36–59.

MacInnes, J. (1998) *The End of Masculinity: The Confusion of Sexual Genesis and Sexual Difference in Modern Society*. Buckingham: Open University Press.

MacKinnon, C. (1982) 'Feminism, Marxism, Method and the State: An agenda for theory'. *Signs*, 7(3): 515–44.

Madfis, E. (2014) 'Triple Entitlement and Homicidal Anger: An exploration of the intersectional identities of American mass murderers'. *Men and Masculinities*, 17(1): 67–86.

Malamuth, N.M. (1981) 'Rape Proclivity among Males'. *Journal of Social Issues*, 37(4): 138–57.

Mangan, J.A. (1986) *The Games Ethic and Imperialism: Aspects of the Diffusion of an Ideal*. New York: Viking Penguin.

Mangan, J.A. and Walvin, J. (eds) (1987) *Manliness and Morality: Middle Class Masculinity in Britain and America 1800–1940*. Manchester: Manchester University Press.

Marsiglio, W. (2009) 'Men's Relations with Kids: Exploring and promoting the mosaic of youth work and fathering'. *Annals of the American Academy of Political and Social Science*, 624: 118–38.

Maxwell, C. (2007) '"Alternative" Narratives of Young People's Heterosexual Experiences in the UK'. *Sexualities*, 10(5): 539–58.

Mead, G.H. (1934) *Mind, Self and Society*. Chicago: University of Chicago Press.

Mead, M. (1935) *Sex and Temperament in Three Primitive Societies*. New York: Morrow.

Melzer, S. (2009) *Gun Crusaders: The NRA's Culture War*. New York: New York University Press.

Messerschmidt, J.W. (1997) *Crime as Structured Action: Gender, Race, Class and Crime in the Making*. Thousand Oaks, CA: Sage.

Messerschmidt, J.W. (2003) 'Managing to Kill: Masculinities and the space shuttle Challenger explosion'. In M. Hussey (ed.) *Masculinities: Interdisciplinary Readings*. Upper Saddle River, NJ: Pearson (217–26).

Messner, M.A. (1990) 'When Bodies are Weapons: Masculine violence in sport'. *International Review for the Sociology of Sport*, 25: 203–21.

Messner, M.A. (2005) 'Still a Man's World? Studying masculinities and sport'. In M.S. Kimmel, J. Hearn and R.W. Connell (eds) *Handbook of Studies on Men and Masculinities*. London: Sage (313–25).

Messner, M.A. (2010) 'Becoming 100 Percent Straight'. In M. Kimmel and M. Messner (eds) *Men's Lives*, (8th. edition). Boston, MA: Allyn & Bacon (371–6).

Miles, R. (1992) *The Rites on Man: Love, Sex and Death in the Making of the Male*. London: Paladin.

Miller, J.D. (2012) *The Generation X Report*, vol. 1(3) on food. Retrieved 16 December 2015 from: http://home.isr.umich.edu/files/2012/04/GenX_Rept_Spring20121.pdf.

Miller, P. and Rose, N. (1990) 'Governing Economic Life'. *Economy and Society*, 19(1): 1–31.

Millett, K. (1972) *Sexual Politics*. London: Abacus.

Mischel, W. (1966) 'A Social Learning View of Sex Differences'. In E.E. Maccoby (ed.) *The Development of Sex Differences*. Stanford, CA: Stanford University Press (56–81).

Moir, A. and Jessell, D. (1989) *Brainsex: The Real Difference between Men and Women*. London: Mandarin.

Monoghan, L.F. (2008) *Men and the War on Obesity: A Sociological Study*. New York: Routledge.

Morrison, M.A., Morrison, T.G. and Sager, C.L. (2004) 'Does Body Satisfaction Differ between Gay Men and Lesbian Women and Heterosexual Men and Women?' *Body Image*, 1: 127–38.

Mort, F. (1988) 'Boys Own: Masculinity, style and popular culture'. In R. Chapman and J. Rutherford (eds) *Male Order: Unwrapping Masculinity*. London: Lawrence & Wishart (193–224).

Muehlenhard, C.L and Kimes, L.A. (1999) 'The Social Construction of Violence: The case of sexual and domestic violence'. *Personality and Social Psychology Review*, 3(3): 234–45.

Mulvey, L. (1975) 'Visual Pleasure and Narrative Cinema'. *Screen*, 16: 6–19.

Murphy, R. (1987) *The Silent Body*. New York: Henry Holt and Co.

Naftolin, F. (ed.) (1981) 'The Dimorphic Brain'. *Science*, 211: 1263–1324.

Nayak, A. and Kahily, M.J. (1996) 'Playing It Straight: Masculinities, homophobias and schooling'. *Journal of Gender Studies*, 5(2): 211–30.

Newman, K.S. (1988) *Falling from Grace: The Experience of Downward Mobility in the American Middle Class*. New York: The Free Press.

Nichols, J. (1975) *Men's Liberation*. New York: Penguin.

O'Brien, M. (2004) 'Social Science and Public Policy Perspectives on Fatherhood in the European Union'. In Lamb, M.E. (ed.) *The Role of the Father in Child Development* (4th. edition). Hoboken, NJ: Wiley & Sons (121–45).

O'Donnell, M. and Sharpe, S. (2000) *Uncertain Masculinities: Youth, Ethnicity and Class in Contemporary Britain*. London: Routledge.

Office for National Statistics (2011) *People in Work*. Retrieved 15 December 2015 from: https://www.ons.gov.uk/employmentandlabourmarket/peopleinwork.

Office for National Statistics (2012) *Lone Parents with Dependent Children*. Retrieved 12 January 2016 from: http://www.ons.gov.uk/ons/rel/family-demography/families-and-households/2011/sum-lone-parents.html.

Office for National Statistics (2015) *Sexual Identity by Region, UK*. Retrieved 25 March 2016 from: https://www.ons.gov.uk/peoplepopulationandcommunity/housing/datasets/referencetable04sexualidentitybyregionuk.

Ortner, S.B. and Whitehead, H. (1981) *Sexual Meanings: The Cultural Construction of Gender and Sexuality*. Cambridge: Cambridge University Press.

Özbay, C. (2010) 'Nocturnal Queers: Rent boys' masculinity in Istanbul'. *Sexualities*, 13(5): 645–63.

Page, E. and Jha, J. (2009) *Exploring the Bias: Gender and Stereotyping in Secondary Schools*. London: Commonwealth Secretariat.

Parsons, T. and Bales, R.F. (1953) *Family, Socialisation and the Interaction Process*. Glencoe, IL: Free Press.

Pascoe, C.J. (2005) '"Dude, You're a Fag": Adolescent masculinity and the fag discourse'. *Sexualities*, 8(3): 329–46.

Pateman, C. (1988) *The Sexual Contract*. Cambridge: Polity Press.

Peat, C.M., Peyerl, N.L., Ferraro, F.R. and Butler, M. (2011) 'Age and Body Image in Caucasian Men'. *Psychology of Men & Masculinity*, 12(2): 195–200.

Philipson, I. (1981) 'Child Rearing Literature and Capitalist Industrialisation'. *Berkeley Journal of Sociology*, 26: 57–73.

Pleck, J.H. (1987) 'American Fathering in Historical Perspective'. In M.S. Kimmel (ed.) *Changing Men: New Directions in Research on Men and Masculinity*. Newbury Park: Sage (83–97).

Pleck, J.H. (1997) 'Paternal Involvement: Levels, sources and consequences'. In M.E. Lamb (ed.) *The Role of the Father in Child Development* (3rd. edition). New York: Wiley (325–32).

Pleck, J.H. and Sawyer, J. (eds) (1974) *Men and Masculinity*. Englewood Cliffs, NJ: Prentice Hall.

Pleck, J.H. and Masciadrelli, B.P. (2004) 'Paternal Involvement by US Residential Fathers'. In Lamb, M.E. (ed.) *The Role of the Father in Child Development* (4th. edition). Hoboken, NJ: Wiley & Sons (222–70).

Plummer, K. (1995) *Telling Sexual Stories*. London: Routledge.

Plummer, K. (2003) *Intimate Citizenship: Private Decisions and Public Dialogues*. London: University of Washington Press.

Pollard, P. (1994) 'Sexual Violence Against Women: Characteristics of typical perpetrators'. In J. Archer (ed.) *Male Violence*. London: Routledge (170–94).

Pope, H.G., Phillips, K.A. and Olivardia, R. (2000) *The Adonis Complex: How to Identify, Treat and Prevent Body Obsession in Men and Boys*. New York: Touchstone Books.

Potts, A. (2000) '"The Essence of the Hard-On": Hegemonic masculinity and the cultural construction of "erectile dysfunction"'. *Men and Masculinities*, 3(1): 85–103.

Pruett, K.D. (2000) *Fatherneed*. Michigan: Free Press.

Radtke, H.L. and Stam, H.J. (eds) (1994) *Power/Gender: Social Relations in Theory and Practice*. London: Sage.

Ramirez, H. (2011) 'Masculinity in the Workplace: The case of Mexican immigrant gardeners'. *Men and Masculinities*, 14(1): 97–116.

Ranson, G. (2012) 'Men, Paid Employment and Family Responsibilities: Conceptualizing the "working father"'. *Gender, Work and Organization*, 19(6): 741–61.

Ray, R. and Rosow, J.A. (2010) 'Getting Off and Getting Intimate: How normative institutional arrangements structure black and white fraternity men's approaches toward women'. *Men and Masculinities*, 12(5): 523–46.

Redman, P. and Mac an Ghaill, M. (1997) 'Educating Peter: The making of a history man'. In D.L. Steinberg, D. Epstein and R. Johnson (eds)

Border Patrols: Policing the Boundaries of Heterosexuality. London: Cassell (162–82).

Reeser, T.W. (2010) *Masculinities in Theory: An Introduction*. Oxford: Blackwell/Wiley.

Reich, J. (2010) '"The World's Most Perfectly Developed Man": Charles Atlas, physical culture and the inscription of American masculinity'. *Men and Masculinities*, 12(4): 444–61.

Reiss, Jr., A.J. (1961) 'The Social Integration of Peers and Queers'. *Social Problems*, 9(2): 102–20.

Rheingold, H. and Cook, K. (1975) 'The Contents of Boys' and Girls' Rooms as an Index of Parents' Behaviour'. *Child Development*, 46, 459–63.

Richer, Z. (2012) 'The Feminization of Labor' in *The Wiley-Blackwell Encyclopedia of Globalization*. Retrieved 17 December 2015 from http://onlinelibrary.wiley.com/doi/10.1002/9780470670590.wbeog201/abstract; jsessionid=33B9A0CFDCFE6A581BEA1BD30E8995D3.f04t02?userIsAuthenticated=false&deniedAccessCustomisedMessage.

Risman, B.J. (1986) 'Can Men "Mother"? Life as a single father'. *Family Relations*, 35: 95–102.

Roy, K.M. (2006) 'Father Stories: A life course examination of paternal identity among low-income African American men'. *Journal of Family Issues*, 27(1): 31–64.

Rubin, J.Z., Provenzano, F.J. and Luria, Z. (1974) 'The Eye of the Beholder: Parents' views on the sex of new borns'. *American Journal of Orthopsychiatry*, 44, 512–19.

Rubin, L.B. (1991) *Erotic Wars*. New York: Harper Row.

Rutherford, J. (1992) *Men's Silences: Predicaments in Masculinity*. London: Routledge.

Rutherford, J. (1988) 'Who's that Man?' In R. Chapman and J. Rutherford (eds) *Male Order: Unwrapping Masculinity*. London: Lawrence & Wishart (21–67).

Rutter, M. (1972) *Maternal Deprivation Reassessed*. Harmondsworth: Penguin.

Sandberg, L. (2011) *Getting Intimate: A Feminist Analysis of Old Age, Masculinity and Sexuality*. Linköping University dissertation.

Scholte, J.A. (2005) *Globalization: A Critical Introduction*. New York: Palgrave Macmillan.

Scully, D. (1990) *Understanding Sexual Violence: A Study of Convicted Rapists*. Boston: Unwin Hyman.

Segal, L. (2007) *Slow Motion: Changing Men, Changing Masculinities* (3rd. edition). Basingstoke: Palgrave.

Seidler, V.J. (1989) *Rediscovering Masculinity: Reason, Language and Sexuality*. New York: Routledge.

Seidler, V.J. (2000) *Man Enough: Embodying Masculinities*. London: Sage.

Seidman, S. (1989) 'Constructing Sex as a Domain of Pleasure and Self-Expression: Sexual ideology in the sixties'. *Theory, Culture and Society*, 6: 293–315.

Seidman, S., Meeks, C. and Traschen, F. (1999) 'Beyond the Closet? The changing social meaning of homosexuality in the United States'. *Sexualities*, 2(1): 9–34.

Seward, R.R. and Richter, R. (2008) 'International Research on Fathering: An expanded horizon'. *Fathering*, 6(2): 87–91.

Shakespeare, T. (1999) 'The Sexual Politics of Disabled Masculinity'. *Sexuality and Disability*, 17: 53–64.

Shilling, C. (2003) *The Body and Social Theory* (2nd. edition). London: Sage.

Shirani, F., Henwood, K. and Coltart, C. (2012) '"Why Aren't You at Work?": Negotiating economic models of fathering identity'. *Fathering*, 10(3): 274–90.

Shuttleworth, R., Wedgewood, N. and Wilson, N.J. (2012) 'The Dilemma of Disabled Masculinity'. *Men and Masculinities*, 15(2): 174–94.

Shwalb, D.W., Nakawaza, J., Yamamoto, T. and Hyun, J-H. (2004) 'Fathering in Japanese, Chinese and Korean Cultures: A review of the research literature'. In Lamb, M.E. (ed.) *The Role of the Father in Child Development* (4th. edition). Hoboken, NJ: Wiley & Sons.

Simpson, M, (1994) *Male Impersonators: Men Performing Masculinity*. London: Routledge.

Slevin, K.F. and Linneman, T.J. (2010) 'Old Gay Men's Bodies and Masculinities'. *Men and Masculinities*, 12(4): 483–507.

Smiler, A. (2004) 'Thirty Years after the Discovery of Gender: Psychological concepts and measure of masculinity'. *Sex Roles*, 50(1): 15–26.

Smith, A.J. (2004) 'Who Cares? Fathers and the time they spend looking after children'. *Sociological Working Papers 2004–05*. Oxford: University of Oxford.

Smith, G. (2008) *The Jamie Oliver Effect: The Man. The Food. The Revolution*. London: Carlton Books.

Smith, B.G. (2013) *Women's Studies: The Basics*. London: Routledge.

Snodgrass, J. (ed.) (1977) *A Book of Readings for Men against Sexism*. New York: Times Change Press.

Solomon, C.R. (2014) '"I Feel Like a Rock Star": Fatherhood for stay-at-home fathers'. *Fathering*, 12(1): 52–70.

Spender, D. (1980) *Man Made Language*. London: Routledge and Kegan Paul.

Stearns, P. (1991) 'Fatherhood in Historical Perspective: The role of social change'. In F. Bozett and S. Hanson (eds) *Fatherhood and Families in Cultural Context*. New York: Springer (28–52).

Steger, M.B. (2013) *Globalization: A Very Short Introduction*. Oxford: Oxford University Press.

Stern, M. and Karraker, K.H. (1989) 'Sex Stereotyping of Infants: A review of gender labelling studies'. *Sex Roles*, 20 (9/10): 501–22.

Stoltenberg, J. (1990) *Refusing to Be a Man*. New York: Meridan.

Stoudt, B.G. (2006) '"You're Either In or You're Out": School violence, peer discipline and the (re)production of hegemonic masculinity'. *Men and Masculinities*, 8(3): 273–87.

Strother, E., Lemberg, R., Stanford, S.C. and Turberville, D. (2012) 'Eating Disorders in Men: Underdiagnosed, undertreated and misunderstood'. *Eating Disorders: The Journal of Treatment and Prevention*, 20(5): 346–55.

Stroud, A. (2012) 'Good Guys with Guns: Hegemonic masculinity and concealed handguns'. *Gender and Society*, 26(2): 216–38.

Sweetman, P. (1999) 'Anchoring the (Postmodern) Self? Body modification, fashion and identity'. *Body & Society* 5(2–3): 51–76.

Tasker, F. and Patterson, C.J. (2007) 'Research on Lesbian and Gay Parenting: Retrospect and prospect'. *Journal of GLBT Family Studies*, 3: 9–34.

Taylor, B. and Behnke, A. (2005) 'Fathering across the Border: Latino fathers in Mexico and the US'. *Fathering*, 3(2): 99–120.

Terry, G. (2012) '"I'm Putting a Lid on That Desire": Celibacy, choice and control'. *Sexualities*, 15(7): 871–89.

Thornhill, R. and Palmer, C.T. (2000) *A Natural History of Rape: Biological Bases of Sexual Coercion*. Cambridge, MA: MIT Press.

Thompson, E.H. (1994) *Older Men's Lives*. Thousand Oaks, CA: Sage.

Thompson, E.H. (2006) 'Images of Old Men's Masculinity: Still a man?' *Sex Roles*, 55: 633–48.

Thompson, J.B. (1984) *Studies in the Theory of Ideology*. Cambridge: Polity Press.

Tiger, L. (1999) *The Decline of Males*. New York: Golden Books.

Tiggermann, M., Martins, Y. and Kirkbride, A. (2007) 'Oh To Be Lean and Muscular: Body image ideals in gay and heterosexual men'. *Psychology of Men & Masculinity*, 8(1): 15–24.

Tincknell, E. (2005) *Mediating the Family: Gender, Culture and Representation*. London: Arnold.

Tolson, A. (1977) *The Limits of Masculinity*. London: Tavistock.

Tosh, J. (2005) *Manliness and Masculinities in Nineteenth Century Britain*. Harlow: Pearson.

Totten, M. (2003) 'Girlfriend Abuse as a Form of Masculinity Construction among Violent, Marginal Male Youth'. *Men and Masculinities*, 6(1): 70–92.

Turner, A.K. (1994) 'Genetic and Hormonal Influences on Male Violence'. In J. Archer (ed.) *Male Violence*. London: Routledge. (233–52)

United Nations Development Report (2014) *Sustaining Human Progress*. Retrieved 15 December 2015 from: http://hdr.undp.org/sites/default/files/hdr14-report-en-1.pdf.

Updike, J. (1993) 'The Disposable Rocket'. *Michigan Quarterly Review*, 32(4): 517–20.

Valentine, G. (1999) 'What It Means to Be a Man: The body, masculinities, disability'. In R. Butler and H. Parr (eds) *Mind and Body Space: Geographies of Illness, Impairment and Disability*. London: Routledge (167–80).

Wajcman, J. (1998) *Managing like a Man: Women and Men in Corporate Management*. Cambridge: Polity.

Walby, S. (1990) *Theorising Patriarchy*. Oxford: Blackwell.

Walby, S. (2009) *Globalisation and Inequalities: Complexity and Contested Modernities*. London: Sage.

Waldner-Haugrud, L.K., Gratch, L.V. and Magruder, B. (1997) 'Victimization and Perpetration Rates of Violence in Gay and Lesbian Relationships: Gender issues explored'. *Violence and Victims*, 12(2): 173–84.

Wallace, B. (2010) *Getting Darwin Wrong: Why Evolutionary Psychology Won't Work*. Exeter: Imprint Academic.

Warren, T. (2003) 'Class and Gender-based Working Time? Time poverty and the division of domestic labour'. *Sociology*, 37(4): 733–52.

Watson, N. (1998) 'Enabling Identity: Disability, self and citizenship'. In T. Shakespeare (ed.) *The Disability Reader: Social Science Perspectives*. London: Cassell. (147–62)

Wee, L. and Brooks, A. (2012) Negotiating Gendered Subjectivity in the Enterprise Culture: Metaphor and Entrepreneurial Discourses. *Gender, Work and Organization*, 19(6): 573–91.

Weeks, J. (1986) *Sexuality*. London: Routledge.

Weeks, J. (2016) *Sexuality* (4th. edition). London: Routledge.

Weeks, J., Heaphy, B. and Donovan, C. (2001) *Same Sex Intimacies: Families of Choice and Other Life Experiments*. London: Routledge.

Weiss, K.G. (2010) 'Male Sexual Victimization: Examining men's experiences of rape and sexual assault'. *Men and Masculinities*, 12(3): 275–98.

West, C. and Zimmerman, D.H. (1987) 'Doing Gender'. *Gender and Society*, 1(2): 125–51.

Wex, M. (1979) *Let's Take Back Our Space*. Berlin: Frauenliteraturverlag Hermine Fees.

Whitehead, S.M. (2002) *Men and Masculinities*. Cambridge: Polity.

Williams, R. (1985) *Keywords: A Vocabulary of Culture and Society*. Oxford: Oxford University Press.

Willis, P. (1977) *Learning to Labour*. Farnborough: Saxon House.

Willott, S. and Griffin, C. (1997) '"Wham Bam, Am I a Man?": Unemployed men talk about masculinities'. *Feminism and Psychology*, 7(1): 107–28.

Wise, S. and Stanley, L. (1987) *Georgie Porgie: Sexual Harassment in Everyday Life*. London: Pandora Press.

Wolfe, T. (1979) *The Right Stuff*. New York: Farrar, Straus and Giroux.

Wolfgang, M.E. (1958) *Patterns of Criminal Homicide*. Philadelphia: University of Pennsylvania Press.

Wood, K. and Jewkes, R. (2001) 'Violence, Rape and Sexual Coercion: Everyday love in a South African township'. In S.M. Whitehead and F.J. Barrett (eds) *The Masculinities Reader*. Cambridge: Polity (133–43).

World Economic Forum (2015) *Global Gender Gap Report*. Retrieved 12 December 2016 from: http://reports.weforum.org/global-gender-gap-report-2015.

World Health Organisation (2005) *WHO multi-country study on women's health and domestic violence*. Retrieved 18 May 2016 from: http://www.who.int/gender/violence/who_multicountry_study/en/.

Yarwood, G.A. (2011) 'The Pick and Mix of Fathering Identities'. *Fathering*, 9(2): 150–68.

YouGov (2015) *'1 in 2 People Say They Are Not 100% Heterosexual'*. Retrieved 21 March 2016 from: https://yougov.co.uk/news/2015/08/16/half-young-not-heterosexual/.

Young, I.M. (2005) *On Female Body Experience: 'Throwing like a Girl' and Other Essays*. Oxford: Oxford University Press.

Zammuner, V.L. (1987) 'Children's Sex-Role Stereotypes: A cross cultural analysis'. In P. Shaver and C. Hendrick (eds) *Sex and Gender*. Newbury Park: Sage (272–93).

INDEX